Warriors on the High Wire

Warriors on the High Wire

THE BALANCING ACT OF BRAND LEADERSHIP
IN THE TWENTY-FIRST CENTURY

Fiona Gilmore

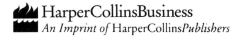 HarperCollinsBusiness
An Imprint of HarperCollins*Publishers*

HarperCollinsBusiness
An Imprint of HarperCollins*Publishers*
77–85 Fulham Palace Road,
Hammersmith, London w6 8jb

www.**fire**and**water**.com/business

Published by HarperCollinsBusiness
9 8 7 6 4 4 3 2 1

Copyright © Fiona Gilmore 2001

The Author asserts the moral right to
be identified as the author of this work

A catalogue record for this book
is available from the British Library

ISBN 0 00 711229 7

Set in Janson and Ellington by
Rowland Phototypesetting Ltd,
Bury St Edmunds, Suffolk

Disney logo used by permission from Disney Enterprises Inc.

Printed and bound in Great Britain by
Clays Ltd, St Ives plc

Contents

Acknowledgements

When I embarked on writing my second book, I expected everything to be easier. I was wrong. However, once again I was lucky enough to have the right mix of people around me who encouraged and assisted me in many different ways in putting this book together.

It is the people who have lent their time, energy, thoughts and enthusiasm to the completion of this book that I would like to thank. The support I gained from them allowed me to focus on my dual roles of author and chief executive of Springpoint.

Special thanks are due to Helena Farrington, my assistant, who to her immense credit took care of the unenviable task of project managing the book, and to my business partner of ten years, Mark Pearce, and senior designer, Roman Huszack, for their advice and creative input.

I would like to thank HarperCollinsBusiness Publishing, and in particular my editor Lucinda McNeile for her invaluable support and belief in this project together with Tamsin Miller for all her hard work in the final stages.

Katrina Symons deserves a special mention. Once again, Katrina joined the project in its primary stage and helped put the jigsaw pieces together.

I would like to take this opportunity to thank the contributors for their incalculable contribution: Giorgio Armani, Karen Edwards, Craig Ehrlich, Michael Eisner, Chris Gent, Gabriel Hawawini, Peter Job, Peter Knoell, Allan Leighton, Jean-Claude Marchand, Jean-Michel Perbet, David Potter, Roger Pride, Achim Schwanitz, Robert Triefus, Malcolm Williamson, Jerry Yang.

My grateful thanks go to: Louise Bahns, Richard Baker, Terry Barwick, Ms Mah Bing Zeat, Tim Brown, Lucian Camp, Christine Castro, Mark Chan, Martin Croft, Kate Ecker, Alison Fennah, Marcus Ferrar, Anne Forrest, Anthony Garvey, Dave Gilbert, Tim Kaner, David Levin, Aldo Liguori, Giles Lury, Lord Ian MacLaurin of Knebworth, Laura Mazur, Caroline McNally, Colin Minton, Becky Rumens, John Ryan, Brian Sharoff, Bill Vestey, Christine Watts.

Finally, I need to acknowledge my special debt to my husband Richard, for reading the entire text and giving detailed comments and suggestions throughout. You have been instrumental in the completion of this book. Thank you.

Contributors' Biographies

Giorgio Armani

Giorgio Armani SpA was established by Giorgio Armani together with Sergio Galeotti in 1975. It was here, in two rooms which they furnished with the money from the sale of their Volkswagen, that his own label of men's and women's ready to wear clothing was created.

Over the past twenty-five years Giorgio Armani's collections have slowly, but inexorably grown. His range has extended from apparel to eyewear, watches, shoes and bags, leather goods, fragrances, cosmetic and home products.

The Italian designer continues to be one of the most distinguished creative entrepreneurs in the world and one whose highly desirable designs continue to be at the forefront of international fasion.

Richard Baker

Richard Baker has been marketing director with Asda Wal-Mart since 1999, with responsibility for corporate marketing, own-label products, customer service and store developments. Before joining Asda plc in 1995, as business unit director for homes and leisure, he worked for Landrover and then Mars Confectionery. Two years after joining Asda he was promoted to deputy trading director with a further promotion to retail managing director of the north-west division following in 1998. In this role he was responsible for forty stores with a turnover of £2 billion and 20,000 employees. He has a degree in engineering science from Cambridge and is married with one child.

Karen Edwards

Recognized as an award-winning brand builder, Karen Edwards is a key force behind developing Yahoo! as a leading Internet brand, and one of the fastest-growing global brands among consumers. Karen joined Yahoo! in January 1996, and formed the brand management team responsible for all advertising, research, promotions, corporate communications and community relations for Yahoo!'s diverse consumer and business audiences world-wide.

Prior to joining Yahoo!, Karen worked at Twentieth Century Fox Home Entertainment as a director of business operations in France, Spain and Italy and as director of marketing for North America. Karen's earlier experience included brand management at the Clorox Company, account management at BBDO for Apple Computer, and public affairs at Chevron USA. Edwards received her MBA from Harvard Business School and holds a BA in communications from Stanford University. Her recent honours include American Marketing Association Marketer of the Year, (1999), *Advertising Age* Interactive Marketers of the Year (1999), *MC Magazine* Marketers of the Year (1998), *BrandWeek* Marketers of the Year (1997), *Advertising Age* Marketing 100 (1996), *Advertising Age* Digital Media Masters (1997).

Craig Ehrlich

Craig Ehrlich has been involved in Hong Kong's communications industry since he first settled in Hong Kong in 1987. He joined Hutchison Cablevision as managing director in October 1987 and was a founding member of the team that launched STAR TV, Asia's first satellite-delivered multichannel television network. After four years with Hutchison Whampoa, Craig was hired as group operations director at Hutchison Telecommunications with responsibility for the company's operations.

In 1993 he left the Hutchison group and established companies which were involved in the introduction of cable television and paging services. He sold these companies in September 1996 and was recruited as group managing director of SUNDAY in November 1996.

Prior to joining Hutchison Cablevision in Hong Kong in 1987, he spent eight years in senior positions at one of America's largest cable television operators.

Michael D. Eisner

For more than three decades, Michael Eisner has been a leader in the entertainment industry, helping to shape this key area of the American economy.

He began his career at ABC, where he rose to senior vice president of prime-time production and development, taking the network from number three to number one with such landmarks shows as *Happy Days, Barney Miller, Rich Man, Poor Man,* and *Roots.*

In 1977, Eisner became president of Paramount Pictures, leading the studio to become number one in terms of both box office receipts and profitability, with such films as *Raiders of the Lost Ark, Saturday Night Fever, Grease, Ordinary People* and *Terms of Endearment.*

In 1984, Michael assumed his current position as CEO and chairman of the Walt Disney Company, and immediately implemented a number of successful growth strategies.

At the theme parks, attendance and revenues climbed due to popular new attractions and the addition of new hotels and an entirely new theme park, the Disney/MGM Studios.

Thanks, in part, to the development of the Disney Stores, Disney consumer products rose to dominance in the field of entertainment merchandise.

The Disney Studios shot from last place to first with live-action films such as *Down and Out in Beverly Hills, Three Men and a Baby, Good Morning, Vietnam,* and *Dead Poets Society.* Renewed efforts at Disney animation resulted in such fiscally and creatively successful films as *Who Framed Roger Rabbit?, The Little Mermaid, Beauty & the Beast, Aladdin, The Lion King, Toy Story, Mulan* and *Tarzan.*

During the 1990s, Disney continued its dramatic growth, thanks to a wide range of initiatives, including:

- The opening of Disneyland Paris, which is now Europe's most popular paid vacation destination.
- The expansion of Walt Disney World with such enhancements as Disney's Animal Kingdom theme park, Blizzard Beach water park, the town of Celebration and the Downtown Disney entertainment district. Further expansions are scheduled in the next two years with entirely new theme parks in Anaheim (California), Tokyo and Paris.
- The acquisition of Capital Cities/ABC, which added the ABC television network and such cable assets as ESPN, the History Channel, Lifetime, A&E and E!.
- The development of such leading Internet sites as Disney.com, ESPN.com, ABCNews.com, ABC.com and Family.com, all aggregated within the publicly traded GO.com tracking stock.

- The acquisition of Miramax Pictures, which went on to release such critical and box office hits as *The English Patient, Good Will Hunting, Life is Beautiful, Shakespeare in Love* and *The Cider House Rules.*
- The creation of Walt Disney Theatrical, which has now produced three successful Broadway shows – *Beauty and the Beast, Aida* and the box office phenomenon, *The Lion King.*
- The development of such theme park-related businesses as the Disney Cruise Line and Disney Regional Entertainment.

Since Michael joined Disney, the company's annual revenues have grown from $1.7 billion to $23.4 billion, operating income has gone up from $291 million to $3.2 billion, and its stock price has risen by thirty-four times.

Michael is the author of a book, *Work in Progress,* which he wrote with Tony Schwartz about his involvement in the entertainment industry.

Born March 7, 1942 in New York, he graduated from Lawrenceville School in 1960 and Denison University in 1964 with a BA in English literature and theatre. He serves on the boards of California Institute of the Arts, Denison University, American Hospital of Paris Foundation, Conservation International, the UCLA Executive Board for Medical Sciences and the National Hockey League. He has established and funded the Eisner Foundation, a philanthropic organization headed by his wife, Jane.

He and Jane have three sons, Breck, Eric and Anders.

Chris Gent

Chris Gent is chief executive of Vodafone Group Plc, and chairman of Vodafone Australia, Panafon (Greece) and other Vodafone Group UK companies. He was managing director of Vodafone Limited from 1985 to 1996.

He began his career at NatWest Bank (1967–71), before joining Schroder Computer Services (1971–79). In 1979 Chris joined Baric Computing Services, where he became managing director from 1983 to 1984.

Chris served as personal political assistant to the Home Secretary in 1974 and National Young Conservative chairman from 1977 to 1979. He is currently a member of Goodwood, the Lords Taverners, Hampshire Cricket Club, Royal Ascot Racing Club and several dining clubs.

Gabriel Hawawini

Gabriel Hawawini is the Henry Grunfeld Chaired Professor of Investment Banking at INSEAD. He is currently the dean of INSEAD (as of September 1, 2000). Previous appointments include the associate deanship in charge of the school's Development Campaign (1998–2000), the associate deanship in charge of the PhD Programme as well as the coordination of the Finance Area (1985–87 and 1996–99), the directorship of the Euro-Asia Centre (1988–94), the directorship of the PhD programme (1998–99) and the holding of the Yamaichi Professorship in Finance (1989–94). Trained in France as a chemical engineer (University of Toulouse) he received his doctorate in economics and finance from New York University (1977). Before joining INSEAD he taught at New York University, the City University of New York and Columbia University (1974–82).

In 1982 he received the Presidential Award for Distinguished Faculty Scholarship at the City University of New York. During the 1987–88 academic year he was visiting professor of finance at the Wharton School of the University of Pennsylvania, where he received the Helen Kardon Moss Anvil Award for Excellence in Teaching.

Gabriel is a past vice president of the French Finance Association (1984–86), a member of the editorial board of several academic journals, and the author of eleven books and over sixty research papers. His publications are in the areas of risk estimation and asset valuation, portfolio management, and the structure of the financial services industry. His recent books include *Mergers and Acquisitions in the US Banking Industry* (North Holland: 1991) and *Finance for Executives: Managing for Value Creation* (South Western Publishing: 1999). He is currently consulting with a number of companies on the implementation of value-based management systems. He has organized, directed and participated in management development programmes in Europe, Asia, the US, South Africa and the Middle East since 1982.

Peter Job

Peter Job joined Reuters in 1963 as a graduate trainee from Oxford University and served as a correspondent in Paris, New Delhi, Kuala Lumpur and Jakarta. He moved into management in 1971 in Buenos Aires and subsequently held a series of posts with managerial responsibility for Asia Pacific, Latin America, Middle East and Africa. He became a director of

Reuters Holdings plc in 1989 after a decade based in Hong Kong in charge of Reuters Asia. He was appointed chief executive in March 1991. From 1989 he was a director and subsequently chairman of the international newsfilm agency Visnews, resigning when Reuters acquired Visnews in 1992.

Peter was appointed a non-executive director of Grand Metropolitan in 1994 and, when the company merged with Guinness, served on the board of Diageo plc from December 1997 to June 1999. He joined Glaxo Wellcome plc as a non-executive director in October 1997 and Schroders plc as a non-executive director in November 1999. Also in 1999, he became chairman of the International Advisory Council of Nasdaq, the US over-the-counter stock market. Other advisory positions include membership of the UK Council of the Fontainebleau-based business school INSEAD (1993), the Department of Trade and the Foreign and Commonwealth Office Business Panel (1998). In December 1995 he became an Honorary Fellow of Green College, Oxford and in 1998 an honorary D. Litt. at the University of Kent.

Allan Leighton

Allan Leighton worked for Mars in a number of sales positions and Pedigree Petfoods as a sales director before joining Asda as group marketing director in 1992. He was promoted to retail director and following a further promotion became chief executive in 1996. He was appointed president and CEO of Wal-Mart Europe in November 1999, following the merger of Asda stores and Wal-Mart. He is a director of a number of companies including Dyson Appliances, lastminute.com and Leeds Sporting plc. He is married with three children.

Jean-Claude Marchand

Jean-Claude Marchand joined Reuters in April 1971 as a sales executive in Switzerland and was appointed sales manager, Switzerland in January 1974. He moved to Singapore as sales manager, South-East Asia in January 1976. In October 1978, he was promoted to sales and marketing manager, Asia, based in Hong Kong. He returned to Europe as manager, Italy in August 1979 and in December 1980 he was promoted to chief representative, West Germany. In January 1982 he was appointed regional manager, Central and Eastern Europe and in January 1984 he returned to Geneva as manager, Central and Southern Region RE. In 1989 he was promoted to managing director, Reuters Continental Europe and became a member of the executive committee of Reuters Ltd in 1992. In January 1995 he became managing director, Reuters Europe, the Middle East and Africa.

He took up his present position in January 1999 and is a member of the group executive committee. He was appointed an executive director of Reuters Holdings plc in October 1996.

Caroline B. McNally

Caroline B. McNally serves as executive vice president, global brand management, Visa International, a position to which she was appointed in 1997. Her responsibilities include developing and managing Visa's global brand strategy, creating brand value communications, maintaining brand and corporate identity standards world-wide, conducting market intelligence and measuring and monitoring world-wide brand performance for Visa. Caroline is responsible for launching Visa's first global advertising campaign targeting borderless segments, such as international travellers. And under Caroline's leadership, Visa's website was designated one of the top fifty sites for online business excellence by *CIO Magazine* as well as the industry's 'Outstanding website' for 1998 by the Web Marketing Association.

Caroline joined Visa in 1990 and has held positions including director of international marketing, communications and destination marketing and vice president of global brand marketing. Her extensive experience in financial services marketing includes positions at American Express and MasterCard International. While at MasterCard, Caroline held the position of vice president of marketing in New York and Paris.

Caroline is a member of the board of the International Advertising Association. A graduate of Vassar College, she received her masters degree in international management from the American Graduate School of International Management.

Jean-Michel Perbet

Jean-Michel Perbet is president and chief-operating officer of Sony Europe. He was born in 1954 in Mâcon, France. After graduating from the IPAG Business School in 1976 he started his career at Texas Instruments.

In January 1985 Jean-Michel joined Sony France S.A. to create their

PC business division. In 1986 he was appointed general manager of the recording media division and in June 1988 he became general manager operations division (IS and logistics). In 1992 he was promoted to general manager consumer products group and was appointed managing director two years later. In 1996 he established Sony Information Technology Europe, and in July 1999 assumed his current roles of president and chief-operating officer.

He is married with one son and two daughters.

David Edwin Potter

David Potter MA (Cantab), PhD (London), CBE, aged fifty-six, is founder, chairman and chief executive of Psion plc.

David was born and brought up in East London, South Africa. In 1963 he took up a scholarship to read natural sciences at Trinity College, Cambridge. This was followed by a doctorate in mathematical physics at Imperial College, London, where he was subsequently appointed to the staff. During the 1970s as an academic, he taught at London University and the University of California, consulted, and published a number of academic papers and a book on the use of computers in mathematics and physics.

Since founding Psion in 1980, David has successfully guided the company through the last twenty turbulent years of the microcomputer revolution. In 1988, he led Psion's flotation on the London Stock Exchange, since when Psion shareholders have seen a return on their investment of 1,400 per cent, in parallel with the substantial growth of the company.

David plays an active role in companies, organizations and institutions outside Psion. He is a member of the London Regional Council of the CBI, a board member of London First Centre and co-chairman of the London Pride Partnership's London Manufacturing Group. He served on the 1997 National Committee of Inquiry into Higher Education (the Dearing Committee), and now serves as a board member of the Higher Education Funding Council for England and on the Committee for Science and Technology reporting to the Cabinet. In the 1997 New Year's Honours list, David Potter was awarded the CBE for Services to Manufacturing Industry. He is married to journalist and writer Elaine Potter and they have three sons.

Roger Pride

Roger Pride is director of marketing at the Wales Tourist Board (WTB). He is aged forty-one and is a business studies graduate. He began his career in the travel and tourism industry with Pickfords Travel. He then moved to Avis Rent-A-Car in a sales-territory management position, initially covering south-west Britain before progressing to the important 'City' territory of London.

Roger then had a brief spell outside the travel industry with Golley Slater and Partners, one of Wales' leading advertising agencies, before joining the Wales Tourist Board (WTB) as travel trade officer in 1985. Since then, Roger has undertaken several roles within WTB and is now director of marketing. He is responsible for developing all aspects of the Board's marketing strategy. He has a particular interest in destination branding and has developed a branding strategy for the WTB which led to the award-winning 'Wales – two hours and a million miles away' campaign.

Achim Schwanitz

Achim Schwanitz is managing partner at Vorwerk, Germany. Achim has spent his entire working life within branded-good-businesses. He began his career in 1968, as product manager at Unilever, Hamburg, before joining Jacobs-Suchard, Bremen, finishing as the chairman of its board of management. In 1985 he became chairman of the board of management at Granini, Bielefeld, followed by a post as chairman of the board at Eckes, Nieder-Olm.

In 1994, he joined Vorwerk, starting as a member of the central executive board. He was promoted to managing partner a year later.

He is currently a member of the Lions Club in Bielefeld.

Robert Triefus

Robert Triefus is corporate vice president of world-wide communications for Giorgio Armani SpA, and has responsibility for all aspects of the Armani Group's global communications including: advertising, new media, public relations, events and corporate international communications.

Robert graduated from the University of Manchester in 1983 and worked as a marketing manager for *Today* (the UKs first, short-lived, colour daily paper) and the *Observer*, before founding his own marketing communications agency. After selling his share in his company he joined the Body Shop, in 1992; working first for the Body Shop International in London as a general manager of communications, before moving to the Body Shop USA as vice president of communications. He was promoted to president of communications in 1993.

In 1994 he left the Body Shop to join Ketchum Public Relations, a US based specialist in global brand marketing, where he was senior vice president and associate director. He left the company to join Calvin Klein as senior vice president of communications, world-wide in January 1996.

Malcolm Williamson

Malcolm Williamson was elected president and chief-executive-officer of Visa International, the world's leading payment system, effective October 1, 1998.

Malcolm joined Visa after having served as group chief executive of Standard Chartered Bank, a major international banking group with operations in nearly 50 countries, since 1993. He joined Standard Chartered's Board in 1989 as the executive director, banking, becoming managing director in 1991.

As head of Standard Chartered, Malcolm led a financial institution that prides itself on innovation, introducing numerous ground-breaking smartcard programmes into the market. Standard Chartered is the first bank in the world to issue a multi-function smartcard based on Visa's Open Platform and Java.

Malcolm was born in 1939. His career in banking began with Barclays Bank, and a succession of management duties led to an appointment as a local director in charge of lending and marketing for branches in north London. Subsequently, Malcolm became an assistant general manager responsible for strategic and operational planning and for management accounting, and then spent three years as regional general manager in London.

In November 1985, he joined the board of the Post Office on taking up the appointment of managing director of Girobank. As chief executive of the Post Office's banking operations, he led the successful development of Girobank up to the point of its planned sale to the Alliance & Leicester Building Society in 1989.

He was appointed non-executive director of the National Grid Group on August 1, 1995, appointed to the Board of British Invisibles on June 10, 1996, elected a member of the Council of the Industrial Society on November 18, 1996, and became UK chairman of the British Thai Business Group on March 6, 1997.

Malcolm is married with four children. His leisure interests include golf, mountaineering, chess and bridge.

Jerry Yang

Recognized world-wide as an industry visionary, Jerry Yang is a key player in setting Yahoo!'s business strategy. Jerry, a Taiwanese native who was raised in San Jose, California, co-created the Yahoo! Internet navigational guide in April 1994 with David Filo, and co-founded Yahoo! Inc. in April 1995. Since that time, Jerry has been instrumental in building Yahoo! into one of the most recognized brands associated with the Internet and a leading force in the new media industry.

A true Internet entrepreneur, Jerry has keynoted and spoken at the most prestigious national and international industry conferences, including Internet World, COMDEX, Spotlight, Jupiter Communications, *Fortune* and *Wall Street Journal* conferences. Both Yahoo! and Jerry are frequently featured in top business publications, including *Business Week*, *Forbes*, *Fortune*, *Time*, *Newsweek* and the *Wall Street Journal*, and appear regularly on key business and financially-oriented broadcast programmes such as CNBC, CNN/fn, C-Span and Fox News to name a few. Jerry serves as an executive officer and is on the board of directors of the company. Jerry also holds board positions on Ziff Davis, Inc., and Yahoo! Japan, as well as sitting on the board for the Asian Pacific American Community Fund, a San Francisco-based non-profit organization. Jerry holds BS and MS degrees in electrical engineering from Stanford University and is currently on leave of absence from Stanford's electrical engineering PhD programme.

Dr Seuss:

Step with care and great tact
and remember that Life's
a Great Balancing Act.
Just never forget to be dexterous and deft.
And never mix up your right foot with your left.

Billy Elliot at his audition at the Royal Academy when asked 'What does it feel like when you're dancing?':

I forget everything . . . I can feel a change in my whole body . . .
I feel like I'm flying . . . it's like electricity . . . yes, like electricity.

Introduction

FIONA GILMORE

When I edited my first book on branding, *Brand Warriors*, in 1997, my major concern was to demonstrate the importance of commitment to brands and the active role of the CEO in managing brand warfare. This was very much in the context of the growing power of retailers and the seemingly inexorable rise in own-label products in supermarkets. While this particular battle is not won, I feel that the importance of brands is now more widely accepted. More and more companies, notably in the US, are recognizing that effective brand management is a key lever in delivering shareholder value. There are other issues now facing the brand warrior.

The title of this book is intended to convey the fact that brand warriors in even the largest, most successful companies face a daily balancing act. The requirements of shareholders for short-term performance, as well as for long-term growth and security, are at the heart of this dilemma. Few brands are ever properly established in a short time frame (although there are some examples in this book from the new technology sector, where powerful brand relationships with the consumer have been built relatively quickly). And even if they are established quickly they usually lack the substance of the great brands which span generations and thus may perish as quickly as they arose.

So judging investment in brand development – which is in so many markets not just marketing expenditure but investment in product development, innovation and service infrastructure – is one part of the high-wire decision making. But that has been part of business life for a long while, even if shareholders are now more vocal and active about corporate performance. On a wider front, the true brand warrior faces other dilemmas. The first of these is how to manage the global reputation of the brand when there are noisy questions being asked about the extent to which globalization represents exploitation of the developing world and destruction of local culture. It is not good enough to say that these questions are being asked by a few demonstrators who are unrepresentative. Global businesses must take the high ground and communicate more positively the benefits of their investment strategy and their policies which prevent exploitation. The second dilemma is organizational structure and the inability of the traditional structures to ensure that the brand is at the heart of the organization – not an appendage tacked on by those nice people in marketing. There is no doubt in my mind that the most successful organizations are adapting their structures to reflect the role of the brand as the core of everything the company stands for. This is particularly important, of course, for service brands when human delivery is the essence of the brand offering. But, in my view, it is no less important in technology brands and traditional product brands, since it requires all of the organization to commit to the brand values in order that the consumer can experience the totality of the brand promise.

We have also seen a massive acceleration in the globalization of business, influenced by open-markets, technology and multinational mergers and acquisitions on an unprecedented scale. This brings huge opportunities but also increases the risk of falling off the high-wire. The sort of international deals of the size of BP/Amoco and Vodafone with AirTouch and Mannesmann were virtually unthinkable a few years ago. They raise huge issues of optimum long-term branding and brand positioning and how best to migrate from the status quo to the chosen solution and over what time frame.

Closely related to this is the managerial challenge of getting the entire organization aligned to a set of cultural values that closely reflects the brand values. More and more of our work on brand positioning shows the benefits of getting this right and the real problems of getting it wrong. I see enormous clarity of purpose and culture in single brand companies which have energized their people. Conversely, some multi-brand companies who lack the unifying force of a single public entity with easily identifiable values and personality are beset by uncertainty and a lack of confidence.

At the level of the individual brand – whether a corporate or unique product/service offering – it is increasingly complex to achieve an optimum brand positioning. For many years, this was the territory of the advertising agency and this can still be true for some individual brands. But a corporate brand requires a much broader skill set: it needs to address different stakeholders with different interests and different levels of sophistication. When these stakeholders cross national boundaries, it is unlikely that any advertising agency has the experience or expertise to attempt the task.

Equally mainstream consultancy firms generally lack the experience and skills to undertake brand positioning work. This is not something that can be learnt at business school or entrusted to the army of number-crunchers that the big firms employ. Brand warriors really do need someone dedicated to brand positioning, whether this is in-house or a specialist brand positioning consultant.

One of the many ways in which such a person can help the brand is by communication equity (CEq) evaluation to establish and measure the key communication equities owned by the brand and their on-going effectiveness. These equities offer the long-term opportunity for differentiation and thus competitive advantage, particularly in markets with little product/service difference.

When developing a positioning strategy for a destination, or anything else for that matter, we have to take account of the macrotrends most likely to influence the customers' needs and moods. One of the most significant macrotrends for destination branding represents one of the key paradoxes of modern society. There is an almost universal need for the emotional 'safety net' of comfort in a world of rapid change, *even for those who embrace technology and change quite happily*. Examples include the renaissance of traditional crafts and food products, the growth of activity holidays and the enjoyment of nature. There is a natural desire to return to our roots when all around us things are changing.

Globalization: the challenge for the corporate brand

While the march of global brands, whether by organic growth or by acquisition, has continued unabated, we have begun to see vigorous signs of some questioning of its desirability. Whether it be protesters in Seattle attacking global capitalism, French farmers objecting to McDonald's or Scandinavians cutting logos from their chic sports shirts, there are unmistakable indications that the corporate brand owner must not ignore the social implications of his actions. It is clear that a significant and growing proportion of the population will be making their decisions about corporate brands on the basis of new criteria, on ethical standards as well as respect and admiration for the product or brand, and the corporate brand warrior must address these issues.

Of course there is a much bigger debate on the extent to which multi-national branding and manufacture exploits the developing world and destroys cultural distinctiveness. But that is outside the remit of this book. My assumption is that global companies will continue to want to invest in the developing world, primarily as an opportunity to offer their products to the populations of these markets and secondarily in certain sectors (for example, clothing) as an opportunity to secure low-cost manufacturing. These ventures will offer opportunities of employment to local people, with advancement and career progression for some, and contribute to the development of local infrastructure in retailing, transport and communication.

However, the key lesson from that debate is that global brand management involves having clear policies which can mitigate the negative impact. Most large multinational companies do have excellent policies and practices, in particular in being good citizens wherever they operate, in spending on housing, healthcare, and education for their employees, eschewing child labour and environmental pollution and so on. But they have not been good at communicating these to an audience beyond their employees and sometimes their investors.

In the future, corporate brand management will have to develop specific communication programmes to ensure that their corporate brand stands high in the consumers' minds for their ethical behaviour and their cultural sensitivity.

In case we get carried away, branding is about enduring values, not about spin to manipulate tomorrow's headlines. Brands must retain their integrity – brand warriors never lie, are never economical with the truth and always prefer long-term gain to short-term pain. Pharmaceutical companies who choose to give medicines to people in undeveloped countries who otherwise cannot afford them may deserve recognition, even if they used this as a PR opportunity. But brands who attach themselves (parasitically) to social issues should be challenged.

Just as there are now, there will always be big international brands and smaller local brands in most categories. The story of SUNDAY – a small local mobile telephone company in Hong Kong – is a dramatic demonstration of how capturing local imagination can make a local competitor more attractive than bigger, multinational names. Neither is better nor worse, just different, and the consumer will make the choice.

Equally, we see in the Visa study an international brand can be perceived as local as well as global. This is partly through its unique distribution through local banks around the world, but also through a consciously local marketing programme overarched by a consistent global visual identity and powerful brand values of trust, integrity and convenience. In the case of Armani, we see a local brand which has grown into a global fashion icon, yet remains true to its Italian roots and the values set out in the personal vision of its founder. There has been no dissipation of these values by a misguided dash for growth.

Organizational structures: transforming them so that the business is the brand

Traditional organization structures are based on a set of departments or functions, reporting to a management board and a chief executive. The marketing function is a separate department, as are customer relations, distribution, research and development (R & D), finance and human resources (HR). As we came into the new millennium my company, Springpoint, conducted some research called 'Wish list' and one of the questions we asked chief executives and other key decision-makers was, 'What is the ideal organizational structure for the future?'

The sample group was 100 key decision-makers and 98 per cent of them were dissatisfied with the traditional organizational structure. 60 per cent envisaged a new structure with the brand at the centre.

Figure 1: A new model for organizational structures

In this diagram you can see how all the departments and functions revolve around the brand. The marketing department is no longer there in the sense that everybody has a responsibility for the brand. At the centre of this new organizational model there are brand strategy and brand direction. Around this core, some of the more traditional aspects of the organization fit in, such as the communications discipline, the customer care discipline and R&D, as well as new product service development and new venture development – all of these functions are involved equally and participate in the future of the brand. This is the kind of structure people are talking about for the future – a structure that allows *everybody to participate in the realization of the brand.*

When you look at the conventional structure of a company you realize how inappropriate it is for the way that brands need to be developed in the future. It was of course the fact that the large fast-moving consumer goods (FMCG) companies structured their organizations in this way and encouraged everybody else to imitate them. In the days when branding was about marketing a product, marketing was indeed just a function, an appendage. That is why when we conducted this research the conventional FMCG companies were cited as being those that were out of touch with the need to build the brand internally. For companies such as Procter & Gamble, where the consumer has not necessarily known the name of the corporation behind the brands Pampers, Pantene and Pringles, they have a number of real challenges in this new world. One of these challenges is how they build a strong corporate brand culture that resonates internally and externally. If they don't have a seamless connection between the two, it is very difficult for the people within that organization to grasp how central the brand is to everything. The second challenge they have is how inspirational their corporate culture can be when the culture in a sense is fragmented between so many different brands. How much easier it is to create real engagement, commitment and belief when you have a single brand and where there is therefore a seamless aspect to the communication between the internal organization and the external communication with the customer. In this sense organizational structure can no longer be separated from the discussion about the brand. Perhaps the implication is that companies such as Procter & Gamble need to ensure that individual brand businesses can draw on a set of coherent values from the parent company to create their own individual brand culture – subtly different for say Pantene, Pampers and Pringles.

So, looking at this ideal organizational structure, one of the benefits is the fact that each employee has to engage with the brand, identify with the brand and be inspired by the brand. I have heard people in conventional FMCG companies saying only recently how there is no connection whatsoever between the internal culture and the spirit of any of their individual brands. They are therefore performing a very difficult task, because they are fabricating something to an external world that has no internal support or validity. It must be much easier to communicate a brand promise where every one is living and breathing that promise every day in their work. Once you have put the brand at the heart of the organization, you no longer regard it as an adjunct. This takes away many of the endless tensions that are created within organizations, where for example, customer service interface and the marketing interface are trampling on each other's toes. The organizational structure has to move from a functional orientation to one that is totally integrated and fluid, to reflect the key drivers of the business at any one time. The Board responsible for the strategy and direction of the brand will be placed at the centre of the organizational structure, not at the top of any ladder or pyramid. At the very centre is of course the customer (or consumer), and that notion of the customer at the centre of the organizational structure seated next to Board management is a useful one.

Does this mean that in the future customers will be playing a more central role? I remember Lord Maclaurin's answer when he was asked what were the key ingredients to the success of Tesco as he strove to transform the Tesco brand, reposition it against Sainsbury's and indeed advance ahead of Sainsbury's. His reply was, 'We listened to the customer every day of the week, every week of the year, we asked the customer's advice, we listened to what the customer liked and disliked. We were never too proud, and we were inspired by our customers' thoughts and ideas as much as our own.'

Understanding that the brand is the very heartbeat of any organization is obvious to companies such as Nike, Yahoo! and Disney. Understanding how you have to change these traditional organizational structures and realize in a sense that every individual within the company is a marketer is one of the biggest challenges for people to face particularly in FMCG corporations.

One of the huge advantages of creating a fully integrated organizational model will be that *everybody* in the organization can understand the brand. A number of the people participating in our research refer to the fact that the majority of people in their organizations did not even understand what the brand was.

Migration strategies: a bit more than changing the name on the door

Between 1991 and 2000, the number of acquisitions recorded in Europe and the US almost doubled, but the value of the transactions, during the same period, increased eight times in Europe and twelve times in the US.[1] This is clear evidence that the scale of acquisitions has dramatically accelerated.

Migration strategies have thus become an item for the board room agenda.

Buying companies is, whatever the lawyers and bankers may say, relatively speaking a doddle. What you do with them once you have acquired them is another matter. The cost-cutting exercises have been considered exhaustively. Synergies in distribution, warehousing, information sharing and R&D have all been analysed and fully evaluated long before the acquisition.

The real challenge, is of course, the brand and what to do with the acquired brands. Banks and financial advisers have traditionally not provided advice on how to integrate different organizations' cultures and how to marry or not to marry together the various brands within the enlarged family.

So many mergers and acquisitions (M & A's) do not succeed.

- 70 per cent of today's mergers and acquisitions fail to deliver expected business benefits
- 70 per cent of those failures occur during post-merger integration
- Only 17 per cent of the cross-border mergers and acquisitions from 1996 to the end of 1998 added shareholder value[2]

The main reasons for these failures are *not* to do with the cost-cutting rationalization exercises. Financial advisers are excellent at making sure that their client companies squeeze the pips, but often 'soft values' are regarded as less important than other issues and this includes brand architecture. Specific reasons for failure include: differences in vision, incompatible culture/brand fit, loss of intangible assets, attrition of talent and capabilities, high co-ordination costs, back office IT disintegration.[3]

We have all seen companies sitting on their acquisitions, allowing the individual brands to continue to build further their own brand equity. The longer these individual brands are left to their own devices, the greater the barriers to bringing them together. The benefits for seeking convergence are not simply the economies of scale derived from marketing communication synergies, but the integration of the best aspects of each culture.

Moving to a single brand, if that is the objective, is indeed a Herculean task, and should not be underestimated by the CEO or anyone else. The challenge is so great that many wonder whether it is viable.

If the business in question is a service-based industry, the objective is to find ways of delivering a similar level of service anywhere in the world. How much easier the task is when you are dealing with product brands. Mars™ became an expert in changing names and migrating product brands, such as Marathon to the internationally chosen name of Snickers. This is a cinch in comparison with the work required to achieve a consistent and acceptable standard of service across frontiers for a hotel group who have acquired another chain, an airline or even a telecommunications company.

In the mid 1990s, when British Airways acquired the French national airline TAT European Airlines the temptation was to perform a speedy operation transforming all the TAT EA branded services to BA. As ever, the real issue was not a technical one, but a deeper concern about the brand values and the ability of the two brands to deliver a similar standard of service. There was a huge dissonance between the two – at the time TAT EA was a very poor carrier, inefficient and lacking on even the basic level of service (an ironic acronym in the English language). BA on the other hand was perceived (at that time) as the most outstanding airline brand, efficient, reliable and offering an exceptional level of service. Strategically, the aim was to transfer the BA brand as quickly as possible across a European stable of brands such as TAT EA. Technically, the task was therefore to introduce the BA brand in a dominant way. However, this would have had a deleterious effect on the BA image, undermining its trust values. Wisely, the decision was taken to endorse TAT EA with the BA brand at a very low level; at the same time, the quality control systems were examined carefully to upgrade the offer as fast as possible. The lesson here is that it is dangerous to take brand architecture decisions in isolation from in-depth knowledge and understanding about customers' attitudes towards the brands in question.

As we can also see from the Vodafone story, the really taxing question is not to do with the definition of strategy, nor to do with the technical complexity, but how to bring together the best aspects of each of the brands and get the people inside on side. When these very people are quite passionate about their 'baby' (because that's the way they talk about creating their thriving business), the act of giving it up, or at least sharing the 'treasure' with others, is tantamount to self-denial or torture. Just as the moves on the chessboard are self-evident to a logical thinker, the business strategy is blindingly clear. The ways in which the new enlarged brand goes forward is the crux of the matter and these ways are not so easy to find. It obviously helps if people throughout the Group share in the planning, development and implementation. In the case of Vodafone, within months the new management team included senior managers from a number of countries. The fact that the home country (in this case, the UK) is not necessarily a blueprint for the future development of the brand is also quite helpful. In place of the feeling of imperialists imposing their will, the leaders can behave with humility and a shared sense of purpose.

Professional service firms such as lawyers and accountants are attempting to provide their clients with an integrated network of companies in key locations across the globe. Premium business is at stake and thus the speed at which they are moving towards a single global brand is great. Some of them are in danger of ignoring the need to move with sensitivity and avoid the risk of diluting brand capital.

The benefits of developing a well-planned migration strategy are significant:

- they can make the point to international clients that each firm is part of the same family, and not just part of a loose alliance of firms
- they allow time for true integration of common purpose and values before moving to the single, global name
- they can minimize risk of losing any equity in the transfer to a single brand
- they demonstrate local sensitivity and understanding for how employees and clients may feel
- they can help to give clarity to the complex issue of visual identity decision-making

There are particular methods of analysis designed to help evaluate the speed at which the company moves towards convergence and the ways in which cultural integration can take place.

Some of the criteria used will include the following:

Figure 2: The factors involved in choosing migration stategy

Strength of local brand awareness	✓ ✓ ✓
Strength of new parent brand awareness	✓ ✓
Strength of local brand predisposition	✓ ✓ ✓
Strength of new parent brand predisposition	✓
Strength of local brand adding new values	✓
Strength of international brand adding new values	✓ ✓
International services – how relevant & to how many people?	✓ ✓
Quantification of international business at stake in the short-term	✓ ✓ ✓
Quantification of local business that may go in the short-term	✓ ✓ ✓

For some organizations the potential loss of premium international business and the value of that incremental business is such that a rapid migration strategy is adopted, sometimes at the expense of local business. These decisions are tough, because the job security of individuals is often in question and the impact of the shift in strategy can destabilize the local brand, causing local clients to shift loyalties elsewhere and employees to leave.

Being part of a larger business and a larger brand can be exciting and very appealing, if handled carefully. The benefits for employees are evident: they have more chance of working and sometimes living elsewhere in the world, they can exchange best practices with new colleagues, they can feel proud to be part of a bigger concern and career opportunities can multiply.

One of the exciting aspects of the Asda/Wal-Mart story is how a range of different cultures are being brought together by a systematic process of communication and exchange of best practice. In fact the cultural differences are not enormous and more national than corporate. The key point is that though Asda was bought by Wal-Mart, the latter recognizes that, particularly in the UK food sector, Asda has things to teach Wal-Mart, so it is not just a case of 'acquirer knows best'.

Internal communications are thus as important as external communications in any migration programme. True alignment of values and objectives will be essential to delivering a newly integrated brand promise. Technical complexities of any migration strategy have to be addressed, but the real challenge is clearly a little more thought-provoking than merely changing the name on the door.

Getting the inside on side: nothing is more important

A debate is raging as to how far internal values need to align with the external brand values; management consultants, brand consultants and other advisers have all been arguing for different points of view.

Over the past ten years a growing body of evidence has emerged[4] to support the view that there are measurable, causal relationships between:

- Employee satisfaction and customer satisfaction/propensity to choose
- Customer satisfaction/employee satisfaction and profitability
- Internal company values perceived by employees and the organization's external reputation

As Colin Minton, a leading practitioner in corporate and employee communications, says: 'without employee engagement (at every level) the brand capital is based merely on marketing hype rather than a sustained reality'.

Inspiring employees to think about the values in the specific context of their day-to-day jobs is the highest priority task for any business leader. The individual employee's ability to deliver the brand promise consistently will make all the difference between a business that merely owns a trademark and a business where the brand capital is constantly augmented.

The success of Vorwerk owes thanks to a brand where the inside is very much on side. Its direct selling methodology depends on thousands of self-employed advisers to deliver the brand face to face with the customer. But it is also interesting to note that the brand extends to its call centre, its appliance repairs and its research and development process.

'Living the brand' has become yet another horrible cliché. Yet, more than ever before, employees' energy, commitment and pleasure in delivering the brand promise to the marketplace is the greatest influencing factor in the sustainable success of the brand. The problem is that whilst most people nod their heads and agree with this sentiment, in reality few things change. Cultural integration and change programmes are often seen to be a distraction from the real business. But only by connecting the internal values with the brand values can it be shown that they are not only one and the same thing but that brand capital, and ultimately shareholder value, will be *enhanced* if there is total alignment. The methods employed to engage employees and gain their commitment usually involve hundreds of workshops on values, attitudes and beliefs. The problem is that the value of these workshops is often dissipated once people return to their normal work routine.

So the new way of assimilating the desired brand values into the whole business requires systems, structures, plans to be produced as a result of a comprehensive gap analysis and a mobilization programme designed to engage hearts and minds of everyone as 'brand capital generators'. In a migration programme, country groups are guided to develop their own models and these are used to build the brand framework for the global brand. The best organizations today recognize not just that unlocking brand capital delivers shareholder value, but that human capital is the only enabler of the process. Brands need committed people who have understood and assimilated the brand values throughout the organisation.

Some of the people committed to the brand may be particularly suited to being the brand poets, who can articulate emotions,

Figure 3: Getting the brand inside, on side

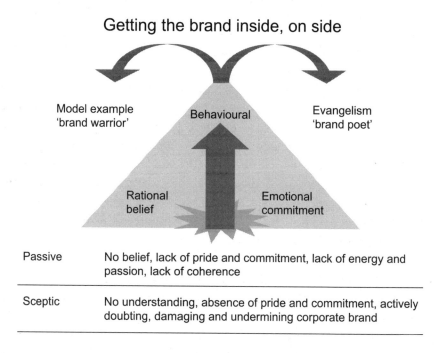

Getting the brand inside, on side

Passive	No belief, lack of pride and commitment, lack of energy and passion, lack of coherence	
Sceptic	No understanding, absence of pride and commitment, actively doubting, damaging and undermining corporate brand	

create vision and dreams of the future. These people need to be encouraged and given opportunities to articulate their vision in a non-structured way. This will rub off on the less poetic and avoid the all too prevalent culture of orthodoxy, sheep-like acceptance and rejection of the original and the unusual. Getting the inside on side means firing up people's imaginations and capturing their hearts, not bullying them into submission. Every brand needs warriors to fight for it passionately and poets to nourish it through the power of their imagination.

Brand positioning in revolution: the new art of brand shifting™

The whole discipline of brand positioning is in a state of revolution. The traditional thinking was that you had a product, you brought it to market and you provided marketing support. You hoped that you would add value to it by developing an emotional proposition and a rational proposition underpinned with differentiating substantiators, wherever possible. This was a seller's world, where ideally you had a superior performing product; you would if you were bold use heavy above-the-line advertising, create impact and interrupt people's TV viewing time with your message. Companies like Procter & Gamble and Mars have pursued such strategies very successfully for decades and have established systems of analysis to refine and perfect their marketing strategies.

Those wishing to make a career in marketing have aspired to join these highly respected FMCG companies in order to acquire such marketing skills, because historically service industries had not, by and large, developed a really deep understanding of brand building and have not therefore been able to train graduates with the same rigour and discipline.

In the last few years we have experienced a revolution in information provision, thanks to Internet and wireless communications. We no longer live in a pure seller's world. The buyer and consumer are now at the top of the pile. We have moved from an industrial society to a service- and information-based society. Consumers are no longer the naive or the ignorant: they are making increasingly informed choices about what they want and what they don't want, how they want it and when they want it.

In a world where conventional product superiority is harder to achieve and almost always transient, brands are less and less about *fixed* product offers and increasingly about ideas. The Halifax Group has launched an online financial services brand called 'Intelligent Finance'. Perhaps before long the people running that business might be tempted to extend it to include 'Intelligent

Shopping', 'Intelligent Travelling' and so on. There is a set of consumers whose interest is in this kind of service. 'Intelligent Finance' is not only concerned with giving real flexibility and choice, but also connecting your savings with your borrowings, in order that the individual can choose if they want to minimize interest payments or maximize savings income. 'We take into account everything you have so you get the most from your money.'

You then have the easyJet brand. This has already been extended into car hire with easyRentacar as well as easyEverything, their chain of Internet cafés. Perhaps they will extend over the years into other territories where ease of use, no-frills service and aggressively competitive pricing appeal to buyers for specific occasions.

In my last book, I talked about Virgin's idea of positioning itself as the 'super champion' of the consumer; Virgin also excels in those service areas where the idea of 'entertainment plus' comes into its own – enhancing the often humdrum experience of a journey or transforming an ordinary holiday into something out of the ordinary. In some consumer research groups, when we asked people what new venture ideas Virgin should explore, the answer came back: 'Virgin Nurses, who would have a fabulous bedside manner, and the University of Life, where you would learn how to work to live, rather than live to work.'

The information age is opening up the scope for brands to spring from great ideas. Now, we are no longer restricted in product terms; we can all use our imaginations and seek to fulfil particular needs more specifically and more accurately than ever before. This is the age for achieving *real* consumer insight and stretching one's creative capacity in finding original solutions.

Disney is, arguably, one of the best-known brands where the corporation focused its attention many years ago on nurturing a core ideology rather than myopically selling a product. Today, Disney continues to extend and expand its brand franchise way beyond its original film product into a host of entertainment and products and experiences. 'Entertainment with heart' is at the centre of its success. Disney continues to give children and adults many hours of pleasure. The creativity that has gone into making this brand such a success inspires many entrepreneurs all over the world.

Disney has understood so well how to evolve its positioning and allow the business to expand around its core ideology. This technique is what I term 'brand shifting'™. The beginning point is a springboard for future business expansion, but brand positioning can shift and move to where the core business will be in the future.

People trained in traditional FMCG business have to re-think their brands' *raison d'être* and explore new positionings for those brands which have had functional or solely product-focused benefits.

For distribution reasons, it is in the interests of FMCG brands to extricate themselves from the total power of multiple retailers and seek out new access points. It is not surprising to see new retail concepts popping up in the UK high street: brands that have historically been cloistered in the traditional major multiples suddenly unleashed on the world, promoting a particular experience and enhancing their in-home product solutions. You have the Lynx cool, adolescent-svengali Barbershop, the Amoy chic spicy noodle restaurant, the Cadbury's calming, warming café, the Nescafé oasis at service stations: each is able to draw on the values of its parent brand but present itself in a new and fresh way. We have even seen the reverse as Pizza Express, for example, sells uncooked pizzas in Sainsbury's. Brand shifting™ is viable for all brands and it is particularly relevant to those who have been stuck in a rut for so many years, fixed in someone else's groove – often that of the major multiples.

The common thread that connects the past with the present and the future has to be the value of each brand – and it, as ever, needs to be distinguishing and go beyond motherhood and apple pie. Also, the emotional hook (once it's found) needs to be maintained and valued and brought to life through more than just the advertising.

When Vodafone first established itself as a player in the UK market its positioning was as the wireless network for corporate use. Today, the positioning is that of the world's largest mobile community. A 'network' is a mechanism. A 'community' combines a functional and emotional benefit. As the Vodafone business expands and extends, brand shifting™ will become the norm. Vodafone was once exclusively an access business. In the future Vodafone will be dedicated to giving access and providing content either through its own services or via Vizzavi, its multi-access portal brand (a joint venture between Vivendi and Vodafone). The new strategic positioning may well be aspirational and a step on from each local brand's current positioning. Certainly, in the case of Vodafone, there was the opportunity to seize the high ground, adopting a very compelling proposition. The communication programme addresses the benefits to the individual of belonging to the world's largest mobile community and belonging to whichever communities the individual chooses ('me and we').

Another example of brand shifting™ in this book is the INSEAD story where its original positioning – as *the European* business school – is being shifted to that of *the global* business school through the opening of a second campus in Singapore. Most importantly, the core value of the INSEAD brand, cultural diversity, makes this shift instantly credible and is virtually impossible to imitate.

We used to talk about brands built on firm foundations. This is still true, but brand shifting™ can develop brands on that secure base. Common purpose and commitment to the values of the brand and emotional reaction provide the base and sense of continuity.

Country/regional brand building: amplification, not fabrication

The marketing disciplines for building brands on a larger scale, such as for a country or a regional brand, are similar to those employed elsewhere, but the challenge is obviously more complex. People within an organization can be inspired to assimilate the brand values into their day-to-day work, but it is another matter when the people of a country are oblivious to the brand strategy determined by a few individuals and not necessarily motivated in any sense to live the brand.

Many factors contribute to the overall proposition – environment, resources, culture, history, economy, and one must not forget the people themselves. The spirit of the people and the spirit of the place are deeply connected. When researching the spirit of Hong Kong, for example, we were confronted with the spirit of the people – their unstoppable energy, their 'can-do' approach to life (*hoh yi*), making the dream a reality. In Belfast, it was impossible to forget the people's *genuinely* warm welcome, their wry and witty *craic* (humour), and their sense of optimism. In Wales, *hywl*, the spiritual yearning for the country, the resilience (from a history of heavy industry and limited income) and the strength of feeling in communities resonate through poetry and music, and in the ups and downs of everyday life. This is not like Italian passion on a hot day in Venice. The Welsh experience more typically takes place on a wet and windy day in Wrexham. It's naturally uplifting, in a bracing sort of way.

All the other contributing factors such as history and environment have influenced this spirit and therefore no brand builder can afford to fabricate it. Political despots are the only men who have ever tried to mould nations and ultimately people return to their natural mores and instincts. Amplification of the most positive assets is, however, a worthy objective and countries such as Spain and New Zealand have been remarkably successful in this pursuit.

A holistic approach to country or regional brand positioning is more effective, but sub-brands can meet more specific needs. Those countries who have developed an umbrella brand for business investors, visitors and residents have achieved impact, but also greater credibility. The spirit of the people and place permeates everything. Yet new propositions tailored to individual target groups can help shift attitudes and explode myths.

Working in Belfast, I realized that the greatest challenge was to refute the stereotypical imagery, mainly stimulated by the stark, uncompromising (often black and white) pictures on the front pages of the press. It was only by being there that one could start to understand the scope and opportunities to be derived from the 'confluence of cultures'[5] – the rich and colourful contrasts in architecture, restaurants and music, for example. Contemporary arts often signal clues to the essence of a people or a place. The Divine Comedy's lyrics not only reflect on the past schism, but also point to the future possibilities 'I was born in Londonderry, I was born in Derry too . . .'

Just as Spain has managed to shed its cheap, tawdry image of the Costa del Boys, Northern Ireland is beginning to celebrate its diversity. A corporate brand can reposition itself relatively quickly, but it can, of course, take a country some years, especially when stereotypical misconceptions are embedded. There are particular concepts that can be launched to speed up the shift in perceptions. In the case of Northern Ireland, for example, 'living history' offers great scope for the imaginative entrepreneur. Rather than shoving the horrors of the Troubles under the carpet, here there is an opportunity to share this history with visitors (and locals alike).

At first sight, it may seem laughable that a country could conceive of having a brand book, that is a formal clarification of the main message, the supporting message and the values of the brand, with illustrations of what works and what does not work. The Wales brand book for instance was given to a wide range of people interested in the future prosperity of Wales – from a bed and breakfast owner in Bridgend to a Japanese investor.

The challenge is to inspire people (to remind them, very often) of these tangible and intangible assets. This is not a question of control, nor is it a straitjacket.

Entrepreneurs who want to connect with the region's brand strategy can focus their ideas on concepts linked to the substantiation of the core proposition. Physical activity holidays such as pony trekking, golf and walking all support the Northern Ireland proposition: 'Touch the spirit, feel the welcome'.

Producing new brand concepts, where the facilities provided are on a par with those of CentreParcs, where the service is available at every level, where the entertainment is that of the region (Irish pubs, Irish music, Irish food ... all being very appealing) – these capital investment ventures are really where the future lies, because the natural, unspoilt countryside fits so well with the desire for a physically demanding holiday. In other words, brand strategies (as ever) are not simply for marketeers – they are for all business people and most importantly for entrepreneurs.

The virtuous circle of destination brands lies in stimulating the private sector to develop facilities, whether they be hotels, restaurants, holiday villages or activity centres, which will reinforce the core message provided by the public sector. Then you really do have a powerful brand promise for the consumer.

E-business: new paradigms, timeless brand thinking

It is no accident, of course, that this book contains a number of examples of new technology businesses since so much of our thinking about brands and brand communication is influenced by the technology revolution. Clearly there is a whole book to be written about e-business marketing but there are some important lessons which are both general and particular.

First, it is clear that one of the reasons for the bursting of the dot-com bubble was the failure of many companies to follow the basic disciplines of brand positioning and brand development, in particular expecting much more rapid change in consumer behaviour than was ever likely.

The founders of Yahoo! did not set out to create a brand, but to provide a service and have some fun. But once they found they had a brand they recruited professional marketeers and made sure that they vigorously protected the integrity of the brand values. These values were transparent and known to all through the induction process: they provided the glue that kept the brand intact through a period of rapid expansion including international development.

The issue of how to optimize innovation is important to all companies and is particularly a problem in technology-led businesses: how can we exploit the opportunities from technology when consumers cannot project themselves forward into a new world? The Psion story provides some useful insights into this process, in particular the need to adapt organizational structures continually to keep idea generation fresh and avoid rigid hierarchies that kill original ideas.

E-business is changing people's lives but not necessarily in the way it was expected to. Most people still have the time to visit conventional retail outlets and *like* doing so. It is only the time-poor cash-rich minority (mainly dot-com millionaires!) who want to buy everything on the Web. But the opportunities, as Unilever points out, in business-to-business and in business-to-employee are enormous. And if e-shopping is not what was hoped, e-information is an enormous opportunity, not least for the ultimate in narrow individual communication with the customer. We also see the emergence of powerful intermediary brands, like Yahoo! and others which enable individuals to obtain more detailed and objective information about rival products, services, or even holiday destinations and to review a wider range of products or services than any other traditional retail outlet could offer. This is giving the consumer more power and choice.

The technical revolution is also enabling traditional organizations to change radically. The Sony story shows how technology is breaking down the traditional boundaries between audio-visual and information technology and is allowing Sony to transform its brand offer along with some powerful product innovations, a radical overhaul of the organization and the development of a truly motivating communication equity – 'go create'. In a very different business, Reuters is using the Internet to transform the nature of its product offering, and is thus broadening its target audience and improving its sales infrastructure, while retaining its core values and appeal to its traditional customers.

Unsexy fast-moving consumer goods companies: they're not so stuffy, after all

The UK major multiples have for many years worked hard to give their customers a rich choice of offers at value-for-money prices. Other supermarket chains in Europe such as Carrefour and Albert Hein have also created attractive environments, a diverse range of products and included a very acceptable spread of high quality own-label products (known as 'private-label' in the US).

For some years now, own-label products have gone beyond being simply poor imitations of the real thing. In the 1990s Sainsbury's introduced a Sainsbury's Saucery range of cook-in sauces, taking Unilever Bestfood's Chicken Tonight head on. Sainsbury's had imaginatively created an appealing name and invested in communicating the emotional proposition. Chicken Tonight was the first cook-in sauce for chicken on the market and so at least it had a head start. We have come to expect serious competition from own-label brands, but have assumed they would never be the first in the market with real product innovation. Now, today, own-label products are threatening their branded rivals, not only on price and emotional promise, but also on innovation.

In February 2001 the Co-op scored a remarkable coup by beating Procter & Gamble and Unilever, the two global giants of the laundry detergent business, in the race to launch the sexiest new product in the market. The Co-op's Brio Actipods are capsules containing premeasured doses of liquid detergent.

Historically, heavy above-the-line advertising would accompany a new brand launch. Own-label would only be able to compete on price.

Today, the world is a really different place. Media fragmentation and the soaring costs of conventional above-the-line advertising mean that an own-label product now has the chance to be the leading brand in a market and at a premium or equivalent price. The private label has a greater chance of appealing to shoppers than ever before, because as Brian Sharoff, chairman of the Private

Labels Manufacturers Association says: 'there are numerous studies including a POPAI survey to show that the majority of purchasing decisions are now made in the store'.

Figure 4: Private label share of packaged goods business

Country	Private label market share/Volume %	Private label market share/Value %
UK	45.4	43.5
Belgium	34.7	26.0
Germany	33.2	27.4
France	22.1	19.1
Netherlands	20.6	18.4
Spain	20.5	14.8
US	20.2	15.8
Italy	17.1	15.5

Source: Private Labels Manufacturers Association 2000 Year Book (A. C. Nielson 1999)

Many European supermarket chains have managed to build their own brand profiles so successfully that their value share is nearly as high as their volume share. In the US there is still a greater focus on the private label's price advantage than in Western Europe.

Wal-Mart is no doubt watching this difference carefully as it develops its European strategy. Asda, its UK supermarket chain, is hugely successful, but that success has been achieved thanks to a number of factors, value for money being only one.

FMCG businesses have to worry about own-label incursion, more than ever, but that is not their only concern. There are other dilemmas.

In the last few years, e-businesses and telecommunications have mesmerized the financial analysts and opinion formers; fast-moving consumer goods have appeared quite the opposite of their name – *slow*-moving, stodgy and staid. Much of this criticism was unfair. However, since the Nasdaq index has fallen so dramatically, the solid FMCG businesses are once again looking more attractive. At least, they're solid. People have to keep washing their hands and their clothes and eating. These things are not vulnerable to the vagaries of fashion.

Yet, FMCG businesses will never be quite the same again. This is meant in a positive sense. The marketing disciplines are still the same, but the scope for new media, new distribution and new venture opportunities has become almost overwhelming. Moving into uncharted waters is scary, but creatively limitless . . .

That's why people at Unilever sound excited. Whether it's the new Cha Teashop, or the Lynx Barbershop, they're breaking new ground. Gone are the restrictions of yesterday's linear product category focus; these brands are now free to fulfil consumers' needs by delivering a service and not necessarily just in the home.

FMCG companies such as Unilever are rationalizing the number of brands to make the most of economies of scale, but also because these brands will become more important to consumers, thanks to their broader offer. Procter & Gamble's Olay was once upon a time just a moisturiser. Now, Olay offers a whole range of nourishing beauty care and cosmetic products. As a result, it plays a more important role in loyal consumers' daily regime.

Unilever has embarked on a migration programme where some of its local brands have been replaced with its global masterbrands. For example, in Germany, the Dante brand has migrated to the Bertolli olive oil masterbrand. In the Netherlands, Royco Soups have been repackaged as Unox, the masterbrand. In Spain, a bechamel sauce made by Amora in France was launched under the Knorr masterbrand. Similarly, in its laundry detergent business, Unilever has successfully transferred the Radion 'sunfresh' concept to its more popular Surf brand. Radion had a market share of around 2 per cent but the new Surf with sunfresh has a higher market share than the old Surf and Radion combined.

Companies such as Unilever have in fact moved very fast over the last few years, harnessing new technology to transform the way they do business faster, more fundamentally than ever before. As Niall Fitzgerald, chairman, Unilever plc says: 'the impact of

Web-based systems on business had been far deeper, more substantial and more strategic than most people would have imagined a couple of years ago'.

In the business-to-business arena, new technology is transforming the way FMCG companies relate to their suppliers, their customers (who are also their competitors). The Internet is enabling Unilever to revolutionize the way it buys. Unilever is expecting to save around 1.5 billion euros between 2001 and 2003 as a result of efforts in this area.

In the business-to-consumer arena, Unilever uses the Internet as a vehicle for building a stronger dialogue with consumers in relevant ways. These FMCG companies are experimenting, partnering, discovering what works and what does not work, with interactive TV wireless communication as well as the Internet. New venture development (NVD) or idea generation is now actively encouraged and many of the new business concepts are springing from NVD initiatives.

Clearly, these activities are crucial to the future – having an NVD model available to every employee on the Web so that they can cut through any bureaucracy is in the interests of a large FMCG corporation. Entrepreneurial communities need to communicate *across* the organization rather than up and down traditional hierarchies.

Ultimately these companies are forging more direct, personal relationships with their consumers, through new technology and new distribution concepts. Traditionally these companies talked about creating dialogue, but in fact it was a monologue. Now, they are really discovering that they can have a dialogue and it's helping them understand better what people want.

Building sustainable competitive advantage through architecture and brand communication equities

Escalating advertising costs and fragmentation of media and distribution channels have forced many companies both to alter their brand architecture and to seek out new ways of having real dialogue with users, purchasers and intermediaries.

Unilever and others have dramatically reduced the number of brands and regard them as brand businesses (inspired by an ideology) rather than category product defined (and limited) brands.

Others have chiselled down to a single corporate brand such as Exel, the global logistics business. Once, they had a whole variety of brands including MSAS, Marken and Mercury. Now they have opted for a dominant single brand, retaining some of the specialist brands as sub-brands, where necessary, at least for the short-term. Organizations such as these have learned to enhance competitive advantage through the creation of architectures, devised to make the most of economies of scale and synergies between customers, employers and markets.

It was back in 1989 that I suggested in an article in the UK publication *Marketing* that companies would have to change and reap the benefits of brand consolidation, moving towards monolithic or endorsement strategies. In my last book, *Brand Warriors*, I chose Virgin as an example of a brand where the brand elasticity resulted from a positioning founded on an ideology, rather than on a product category definition.

Some companies have failed to take steps to use architecture as a means of achieving greater synergies. United Biscuits had bought a number of bakery specialist companies across Europe, well-known names in their local markets, such as Verkade (Netherlands), Fazer Biscuits (Finland) and Oxford (Denmark). Rather than moving swiftly to transfer their brand capital into one single name, they were left to continue to invest even more capital in their local name, thus creating a bigger barrier to any future change. They woke up to the real challenge in 1999. It was too late. In 2000, Nabisco and Danone seized the opportunity to share out the valuable brand spoils by breaking up the United Biscuits business. United Biscuits was crushed to crumbs, a sad day for all those at the company who had worked very hard to build some of the finest bakery businesses in the world. Synergies in purchasing, trade distribution, operations, R & D and new product visioning are crucial, but without the accompanying brand synergies, there is no validity in a common purpose and shared values – no chance of maximising communication economies of scale and impact.

The United Biscuits story is reminiscent of the Rowntree case, where they had established an enviable raft of popular product brands including Yorkie Bar, Smarties and many others, but the brand synergies that could have accrued from the use of the Rowntree name were neglected. On acquiring the Rowntree business, Nestlé moved at the speed of light to endorse all these confectionery businesses with their Nestlé brand.

The most dramatic change in any market must surely be in the financial services arena. Banks and insurance companies are taking the idea that 'the show must go on' very seriously, whatever brand conundrum has yet to be sorted out behind the scenes.

As HSBC and AXA have scooped up local brands, their challenge is to find shared values that come from their own people and yet are also motivating to customers. It is their chance, as it is for Vodafone, to take the high ground and choose a benefit that, thanks to their capabilities, they really can deliver. There is an opportunity here as the requirements of customers from financial institutions vary very little between countries and thus banks and insurance companies can have some global brand values. The exploitation of this (as we have discussed earlier) does not fall on one person within the organization, but is everyone's responsibility.

Creating international trademark awareness through advertising and sponsorship is relatively straightforward. The real challenge lies elsewhere. Lucian Camp, financial services communications adviser, says, 'How on earth this back-fitting approach could ever be successfully adopted within enormous, multi-site, multi-service, multi-market businesses is quite literally impossible to imagine . . .'. I would not be so ready to pass judgement. Yes, the jury is out. If these consolidating brands can find an optimum brand differentiation and find imaginative and effective ways of assimilating their brand values into their business plan, I can see no reason why this approach cannot work. The problems occur when people believe this issue is purely one for the marketing department.

There are notable examples of alternative architectures to the monolithic choice made by AXA and HSBC. GE has for many years successfully adopted a dominant endorsement strategy. Others such as Zurich (financial services) appear to approve of this principle and are attaching 'Zurich' to a range of brand names.

Some local country brands are opting for alternative architectures allowing their portfolio of brands (often as many as ten consumer-facing ones) to concentrate on particular markets, specializing in particular service lines. It is often by no means clear whether the policy to retain a portfolio of brands was a deliberate strategic intent of an acquisition or a post-hoc, line-of-least-resistance policy decided after the event. As Lucian Camp says, 'The story so far is that many of the brand portfolios have run into some sticky problems.'

Some of these problems have occurred because their new brands have been driven by managers coming from the original 'institutional' brand where there was limited scope for the single-minded commitment, clarity of vision and passion that can only come from total immersion in the values and the purpose. Internet-based financial brands, for example, proliferated in the mid to late nineties. They were sometimes technology-led (people momentarily mesmerized by bells and whistles) rather than by a penetrating consumer insight. In the UK, there is a seemingly inevitable move towards consolidation and the worry is that managers have only paid lip-service to brand strategy, and have concentrated instead on distribution and cost-cutting exercises.

Whilst the brand portfolio approach appears expensive, there are some success stories emerging. Halifax did not attach its name to St James's Place Capital (previously J. Rothschild Assurance) in rather the same way that Wall's Ice Cream has not attached its brand marque to Ben & Jerry's (at least in the short-term).

Local brands and local heroes may disappear as the overwhelming power of the global brands becomes all-consuming. Their hope is that as customers become more selective and more discerning, the personalized service benefits developed by them will engender loyalty. Co-operative and building society brands may be particularly compelling as the antithesis to the global monoliths.

In my recent discussion with Lucian Camp, he concludes (presciently, perhaps): 'There were over one hundred brands in the UK automotive industry in 1950, and no doubt at that time an equivalent analysis could have been made of their various brand development strategies. Today, that would be a document of only the vaguest academic interest.'

Competitive advantage can be further strengthened if the brand has a whole *bank* of communication equities. Conventional wisdom has suggested that the communication equities (CEqs) are simply logos. So, up until a few years ago, the world of copyright revolved around brand name and logo protection.

The notion of sweating the assets is well-known to most, but the idea of sweating the CEqs is still not understood by many CEOs and finance directors. I only know a handful of companies who carry out comprehensive CEq audits, exploring the value of established CEqs, the full potential of existing and new CEqs as well as the synergies between them.

The starting-point is as ever the brand essence – its core ideology. A rich tapestry of ideas may be expressed, constantly regenerating and reinterpreting that simple idea. These ideas could involve literally any form of expression using all the sensory responses – sight, sound, touch and smell. The CEq bank multiplies its investment, all the time.

Disney's ideology of 'making people smile' is refreshed and reinvigorated through the service, the characters and the physicality of the world created.

Goldman Sachs' 'unrelenting thinking' is not an empty advertising claim. Every Goldman Sachs employee that one has come across has an iron-like grip on this concept. The logical conclusion suggested is that 'unrelenting thinking' leads to 'unrelenting money-making'. Certainly, Goldman Sachs appears to deliver the end promise. The rigorous ability to filter and cut through, the manner of the employees and the office environment all combine to reassure their customers and partners of the quality of this premier league team.

Invisible services such as wireless communication are working hard to *materialize* the brand: not only through high street retailing, but also in the way the promotional material is executed. Orange fascinated and intrigued the European customer from the outset by creating a bank of CEqs even before its service could actually deliver the full promise. The slogan 'The future's bright' suggested that this network would deliver something better and attracted young people as well as many 'high achievers' and 'explorers' to their brand, casting a metaphorical shadow over the competition. The use of the colour orange and the way the brand was illustrated created a beacon, symbolizing the feeling of optimism in this new exciting era. Vodafone's development of its 'speechmarks' identity was a way of capturing the richness and variety of human discourse – the ability to change ideas whoever you are, whatever you do, wherever you happen to be. Vodafone will realize the full potential of this concept through its global advertising and other communications.

The twenty-first century's pace of change and competitive aggression will necessitate the establishment of CEq banks. At the very least people will register and protect CEqs prior to the evolution of any actual service. As a consequence, trademark attorneys will have a field day; companies are investing in their futures, realizing that the ownership of a range of equities from single words, sentences, particular combinations of colours, packaging shapes, materials, website sound identifiers, photographic styles as well as the conventional corporate identity components will feed their brand, ultimately augmenting its capital.

Not every CEq will be direct communication in the conventional sense. Some will touch people deeply and yet achieve their effect more by osmosis than by hard sell. For example the film *Braveheart* attracted more visitors to Scotland than any conventional advertising campaign. A newspaper photograph of Mick Jagger drinking Highland Spring mineral water in the mid 1980's helped the brand acquire cult status in a way that is hard for advertisements to do. In the US Halls cough lozenges are offered free at public concerts ('Silent nights at symphonies'). The trick is to find new ways of connecting with people's dreams and needs, continuously and imaginatively.

That is one of the reasons why companies need to get all their partners on board – brand consultants, corporate identity designers, PR advisers, direct marketing and advertising agencies need to work together as a 'kitchen cabinet' to interconnect these equities. A partner rather than supplier approach makes more and more sense, as the challenge is to build sustainable CEqs, within a single framework that springs from one core brand ideology.

Conclusion

Brand warfare gives the same switch-back ride, alternating between exhilaration and disappointment, that has been the characteristic of physical warfare through the ages.

Brand warriors live on the high wire as they seek to grow, explore new markets, develop new techniques and create a few useful ideas. Brand warriors, like chess grand masters, never stop learning, and the problems they face become more complex and difficult as the world around them changes. We have learnt a lot putting this book together: I hope you will learn, whatever your company size or discipline, more of the excitement of effective brand warfare in the twenty-first century.

1. Thomson Financial Securities Data, March 2001.
2. KPMG.
3. IMD.
4. *Harvard Business Review*, Mar/Apr 93, 'Loyalty based management', by F. F. Riechheld, W. Earl Sasser; *Harvard Business Review*, Mar/Apr 94, 'Putting the service – profit chain to work', by Heskett, Jones, Loveman, Earl Sasser, Schlesinger; *Harvard Business Review* Nov/Dec 95, 'Why satisfied customers defect', by T. O. Jones and W. Earl Sasser Jnr UPS – HBS; *Harvard Business Review* Mar/Apr 96, 'Learning from customer defections', by F. F. Riechheld, W. Earl Sasser.
5. Michael Longley, 'Tuppeny Stung', Belfast, Langan Press 1994.

1 | Armani: The Cult of the Fashion Brand: Defining Style Across Six Continents'

Based on an interview with ROBERT TRIEFUS,
corporate vice president

In the ephemeral world that is fashion, few designers last the course. Even fewer manage the task of maintaining their brand's relevance for an extended period: keeping the consumer hungry for almost anything they produce. Taste, style and sheer whim must all be factored into any equation involving a business in which the core proposition is fashion. Yet mention the name Armani and a mass collective memory will summon up images of understated urban elegance probably coupled with the term 'modern classic' and the notion that this is a brand that has been around almost forever. It is also highly likely that a picture will form of Giorgio Armani the man, a mystique centred upon his lifestyle and on Italy as a whole.

The story of the Armani brand is one of a svengali-like series of transformations, keeping one step ahead of an easily fatigued consumer and at the same time presenting a public face of apparent seamless continuity. As a customer-focused company, with many different sub-brands, the phrase 'giving them what they want' is more easily applied to Armani than to most.

Understanding how this has been achieved is an object lesson in brand maintenance and the enduring power of a truly global aspirational brand.

An *Italian* icon

Although the name Armani is associated today with Italy and more particularly with Milan, this hasn't always been the case. Milan has only held its Italian fashion crown since the middle of the last century and the Armani brand is a far more recent phenomenon than this.

Giorgio Armani's introduction to fashion took place after military service had taken him from a brief interlude as a medical student at the University of Milan to the nearby town of Verona. Here he was influenced by the operas that are so much a part of the cultural baggage of that city. If you want to watch opera, Verona is one of the best places to do it, as it has the Roman arena for the summer and an opera house for the winter. Watching grand opera caught his imagination and it was probably here that he first formed his love of clothes – looking at the richness of the costumes and the singers performing is similar in many ways to viewing an Armani collection unveiled on the catwalk.

Giorgio Armani left Verona for Milan in 1957. Milan at that time was already beginning to assert its position over other Italian cities as the centre of fashion and when he was offered a job as an assistant photographer at the local department store La Rinascente, he readily accepted. It is important to realize that at the time La Rinascente was somewhat more than just a department store. In effect it was a space for cultural events and initiatives and it provided him with a platform to come into contact with a broad spectrum of creative talent. Armani was fortunate and learnt the retail trade working as a window dresser before eventually being transferred to the Stila Moda Ufficio (the fashion and trend office) where he took charge of menswear buying for the store.

Meeting and working for Nino Cerruti in the early 1960s was a formative time for Armani. Cerruti tested his instinct for fabrics and design on several occasions until finally Armani was able to design a knitwear and shirtings range for his Hitman collection in 1964. It was important for Armani to understand how the retail and couture businesses worked as he lacked formal training. But by 1966 he felt sufficiently confident to launch his own collection, assisted by his future business partner, Sergio Galleoti. Galleoti's instinctive business acumen and marketing skills were to help Armani when he left Cerruti and became a freelance fashion designer in 1970.

At this point, it must be borne in mind that Armani had still not designed anything under his own name, although he had gained considerable experience of the Italian fashion industry. In fact, it was not until 1975 that Armani launched the company Giorgio Armani SpA, which he owned jointly with Galleoti. As happens to many designers, he had decided it was time to go it alone. Armani was forty, quite old by the standards of the design world, but it seemed to him that he had a 'point of view' that needed to be expressed.

He launched Giorgio Armani as a brand centred upon a menswear collection. This was an unusual move at the time: womenswear was the normal initial point of entry to the industry. But the turning point for Giorgio Armani was to come shortly after this when he started working on what was to be soft unstructured tailoring. He had always thought that structured tailoring was fine, but there should be an alternative. The unstructured jacket was something that gave him a real point of difference and which was accepted very quickly, particularly in Italy. At the time, it was considered a minor revolution and as a style of dressing it has been copied ever since. Being the first to do this makes it a seminal moment in the birth of the brand. The Martin Scorsese film *Made in Milan* (1990) in which Giorgio Armani takes a jacket and literally rips it to pieces, laying bare the linings and the method of construction, is perhaps an indication of the way the outside world viewed the change of emphasis. He had the opportunity to do something new: a chance to more or less invent a casual, free-flowing style without formal structure. Over time this has become emblematic for the brand as a whole.

The film *American Gigolo* in 1980 certainly helped to put Armani onto the global stage. It starred Richard Gere, dressed throughout in Armani, and it was big news at the box office. Obviously the choice of clothes for the film was the director's, but it was the concentration upon how Gere looked and the consequent show-casing of the Armani collection that was so important. The film became a reference point for men's dressing in the early 1980s and this played a powerful part in confirming the brand's position.

Brand values

As to what the brand represents, early on Armani took many of the concepts of men's dressing and offered them to women in a way that had not been done before. This gave the brand its distinct point of view, setting it apart from other fashion houses. With the benefit of hindsight, this has served Armani well. One of the challenges in fashion is how to remain current and Armani's brand proposition has never been about being cutting edge. It has certainly never been about being avant-garde just for the sake of provocation. It is more about style and creating clothes that make people feel comfortable, make them feel confident. So Armani is not at fashion's margins; its position is more towards the centre.

It is very important not to underestimate the 'Italian-ness' of the Armani brand. This is a brand that is one of the best known, if not the best known, fashion name in the world and it is uniquely associated with Italy. This brings with it the idea of quality. The Armani name stands for quality at all levels and customers buying from the collections believe this.

Armani clothing is not about decoration. There is an essence of minimalism, but not to the point of total abstraction; this is minimalism with *luxury*. The fabrics, the cut and, of course, an obsession with detail are all part of the brand proposition. From this perspective Armani is very different from a French couture house. French style is much more about dressing up and ornamentation, in contrast to the Armani preoccupation with function. The brand does mean style and elegance, of course, but for Armani the clothes must, above all, be wearable.

The difference when you wear Armani is that you want to look good but you don't necessarily want to make a lot of noise about it. Of course, Armani also instils the *dream* element into his fashion, but through the choice of fabric, the elegance of the cut and the quiet sophistication of the colour. Giorgio Armani wants his customers to feel special when they wear his designs, be it a suit, a sweater, an evening gown or even a pair of sunglasses. He embodies the brand and its values himself – in the way he dresses and lives. This is not about suits: it is about creating the lifestyle that means the brand will be desired. One of the reasons that the Giorgio Armani name has been so closely associated with celebrities and Hollywood is that it is important for Armani to be seen as glamorous. Armani has provided the clothes for over one hundred films now and the bond between brand and cinema is very well established, putting Armani in a very particular place with its customers.

Brand evolution

In many ways the evolution of the brand has been similar to that of other designer-led houses. They have all had a seminal moment where they have transitioned from small-scale, family-style companies to being larger scale 'businesses'. They then need to mature and reach a critical mass, but if you speak to any of the big fashion names today, it's generally been about intuition as they have gone along. Intuition rather than market research has played a strong part in the development of the biggest names in fashion today, however this is now changing as the brands become global and the stakes become higher. A defined brand strategy is now de rigeur for the big fashion groups.

The history of the best known fashion companies shows that they have been run for the most part jointly by a designer and a business partner. Sergio Galleoti, Giorgio Armani's business partner when he started the brand, tragically died in the early years of the company's evolution leaving Armani to oversee both design and business development. The success of the brand speaks for itself as a testament to Armani's strength as a designer and an astute businessman. A steady prudent approach to growing the brand has ensured that Armani has not fallen victim to the urge to seek rapid expansion at any cost, as some other designer brands have done. As a direct result the Armani name today is a gilt edged world-wide brand.

Brand structure

The brand structure itself needs some explanation. There are a number of key values that are communicated to an Armani customer and which will be common to all the sub-brands. Quality, style and modern Italian individuality are the guiding master-brand principles and Armani's brand guardians strive to maintain these in every aspect of the business.

At the top of the pyramid there is Giorgio Armani, the black label. This is the most expensive and luxurious part of Armani and is targeted at a sophisticated, modern and very affluent clientele. This customer is probably in the 30–50-year-old age bracket, and the brand has quality and luxury as touchstone differentiators. This is showcase territory where the collection borders on haute couture. In practice it means that a limited number of customers and a correspondingly narrow distribution pattern are apparent. It is also the original Giorgio Armani brand that was launched in 1975.

Directly beneath this sits Armani Collezioni, the white label. This is a business and casual wardrobe for an aspirational career-minded customer. It is a 'diffusion' line, meaning that it is less expensive than the black label, putting it within the reach of a broader audience. Some customers think they are buying Giorgio Armani when they buy from Armani Collezioni. The emphasis is very much upon the Italian heritage of the brand and it is highly aspirational.

Below Armani Collezioni is Emporio Armani, a sub-brand for a younger and more urban customer. Targeted at the 25–40-year-old, its aim is to be confident and cosmopolitan. Emporio Armani is what you sometimes hear referred to in the United States as a 'bridge line'. It is called a 'bridge line' because it represents a step up for those who aspire to white label ownership but who cannot necessarily afford it. As a strategy, 'bridge lines' have varying amounts of success and by no means all of them have worked. But sometimes they do succeed; for example, without her DKNY 'bridge line' Donna Karan would have no business. However Emporio Armani today has become a global brand in its own right with over 130 free-standing shops located in all of the important world capitals.

At brand entry level, the bottom of the pyramid, are A/X Armani Exchange and Armani Jeans. Both brands occupy the same niche, but A/X is distributed in the US and Asia Pacific, while Armani Jeans is a mainly European proposition. A/X is a line of basics but with an Armani design twist. The reason it has become so successful is that it is street fashion at an accessible price with a designer name.

Once those central brand lifestyles have been established, then you decide what is appropriate in terms of a product range. Whichever sub-brand you happen to look at, there will be a consistency of approach; this is vital to Giorgio Armani. If you look back over the last twenty-five years there is a real thread that ties everything together. Even when Armani has had a season that may not have been critically acclaimed on the runway, customers continue to buy because they know what Armani stands for. In the final analysis, any brand is about the customer rather than the designer and Giorgio Armani always tries to keep this in mind. Each of the sub-brands underlying the Giorgio Armani master-brand is about product diversification. Beneath each of the sub-brands, the business development strategy involves building product portfolios and lifestyles. Giorgio Armani continues to do this. In 2000 he launched Armani Casa, a collection for the home, which is now available in free-standing Armani Casa stores in Milan, New York, Los Angeles, London and Athens. The year 2000 also saw the introduction of Giorgio Armani Cosmetics as part of a constant stream of product diversification, but always within the boundaries of the master-brand.

Building a global brand

As has been said, the central philosophy of the Armani brand has been to grow methodically year-on-year and this helps to avoid some of the problems that result from over-distribution. The pressures of the stock market have driven other designer brands to seek accelerated expansion through licensing and franchising. Giorgio Armani has shunned the possibility of a flotation, instead opting for a strategy of organic growth, placing a premium on product quality and optimum distribution.

Armani believes that you have to control your business absolutely and the house has been effectively acquiring those parts of its business that it had not owned in order to effect this. This policy is being applied across manufacturing, distribution and retail. It is clear that the more you license your brand, the less control you have over it. Control brings consistency. This is critical for any global brand and Armani, with its high-impact advertising campaigns, unique entertainment industry connections and defined retail store concepts, demands world-wide consistency throughout.

Then there is the question of the personality behind the brand and brand longevity. Armani is aware that his name will outlive him. He tries to provide motivation and communicate a sense of vision to those he works with, but he is always looking at how the brand will continue to evolve when he is no longer part of it. To this end, the Armani Group now has regional companies managing the business in Europe, North America and Asia Pacific and there is a strong executive management team base at the company's headquarters in Milan.

Brand sentries – the brand in the retail environment

As Armani is so customer focused, the retail presence is fundamental in confirming the image of the product that people expect. Armani does sell to some department stores, mainly in the US, Japan, France and the UK – where department stores work. However the main focus for Armani is its own exclusive network of retail stores, which are designed to reflect the specific image of each of the separate lifestyle sub-brands.

E-commerce will also be part of Armani's future. You can already buy A/X through the Internet – in America only at the moment.

But for a luxury brand, the top end customers who are willing to pay \$2,000–3,000 dollars for a suit want to be able to go into a store and have the experience of feeling the fabrics, trying the product and receiving the personal attention of a sales representative. So Giorgio Armani's view is that at the top end e-commerce does not have major relevance. It will support and complement the brand, but will not replace the stores. As an alternative distribution channel and another way of fore-grounding the brand, the Internet is efficient and it is for this reason that Armani has invested substantially in one of the most comprehensive websites in its sector.

In terms of brand guardians, anyone working for a brand will know that the only way you can successfully defend a brand is by recognizing its values. Whether it is in the advertising, the PR or the packaging, everyone realizes the importance of this. This means that there are custodians throughout Giorgio Armani: from the person who sells in the store right the way up to the designers in Milan. It is largely a question of sharing a common set of values, living the brand and the dream.

Learning from mistakes and the future

Over its twenty-five-year history the Armani Group has learned from its experiences. A/X when it was launched was incorrectly positioned. The product was not well defined and the price point was wrong, but following a series of strategic changes the sub-brand is now flourishing and offers one of the most exciting areas of development and growth for the company.

Another example would be perhaps the accessories business – shoes, bags and small leather goods. As much of what Armani does is aspirational, having accessories is an important component of the business. Accessories are a more accessible entry level to the brand for many people, and it gives them a slice of a lifestyle at an affordable price point. It is very much about giving access to the Armani brand, and this is something that Giorgio Armani is now trying to do. Perhaps you could look back and say that as a strategy Armani should have been focusing on growing the accessories part of the business sooner. In 1999 Armani announced a major initiative to expand this segment at a rapid pace with the establishment of a new infrastructure dedicated to the accessories business and a mission to open accessories-only retail stores, the first of which is now open on Milan's Via della Spiga.

Commentary

As you arrive at Milan's Linate Airport and the shuttle bus carries you towards the terminal, a vast billboard on an aircraft hangar catches your eye: Emporio Armani. You haven't even had the chance to clear customs before the primacy of the Armani name is apparent. Milan and Armani are today almost synonymous. It is a feat that has not been realized overnight, but which has happened in a gradual, organic manner, in many ways mirroring the progress of the brand from its beginnings in 1975.

Organic the growth may have been, but it has been the promotion of the Armani name in the worlds of cinema, music and high culture that has given it the boost it required to achieve its phenomenal growth and pre-eminent position. Unlike many other brands that have come and gone, the Armani name remains intact and the association with quality, luxury and a particular Italian view remains undimmed.

This success has been achieved though attention to detail and a general willingness to do things differently. Ever since Armani's decision in 1980 to show his collection in a *palazzo* rather than at the traditional *alta moda* in Milan, this has been a story of gentle rule-breaking combined with product and brand consistency: a true velvet revolution. 'Living the dream', while it may be something of a cliché in branding terms, is a reality for those within Armani and it is successfully communicated to Armani customers, giving continued strength to the brand.

Equally, as a global brand, Armani pulls off the trick of not appearing to be pushy while remaining ubiquitous. In whatever context – film, the arts, or the high street – it is almost impossible to avoid some reference to the brand, and as a household name it has become a benchmark of Italian sophistication and understatement. Given this and the brand's ability to reinvent itself, capturing the zeitgeist, there is no reason to suppose that the next twenty-five years will see any reversal in corporate or brand fortunes.

2 | Disney: Managing a Magical Brand

MICHAEL EISNER, *chairman and chief executive*

There can be few individuals on the planet who have not been touched by some part of the Disney brand. Its animated films have made it one of the truly great icons of the twentieth Century. But now that the brand spans films, television, leisure parks, hotels and cruise ships, how does it maintain its values, integrity and relevance? Its chairman and chief executive officer Michael Eisner explains.

When I first came to Disney in 1984, as chairman and CEO, I was more than just a little awestruck. I had spent my entire career in the entertainment industry, most of it at two companies – the American Broadcasting Company (ABC) and Paramount Pictures. Suddenly, I found myself at an entertainment company that was distinct from any other. This was because the company's name – Disney – meant something. Consumers expected something of it. It was a brand.

Unfortunately, my reverie at getting to oversee the Disney brand came to an abrupt end when I realized that it was now my responsibility to keep it thriving. After all, a strong brand alone does not assure success. I'm sure there were some really great brands of buggy whips at the turn of the century. Then the automobile came along.

If I was to serve as a good steward of the Disney brand, I realized I'd better first get to know it intimately. And so I learnt the first rule of brand creation: it helps to be a genius. This is clearly what Walt Disney was. And it helps to have someone who is also brilliant to help manage the fruits of that genius . . . and, it's even better if that person is your brother – in this case, Roy Disney – who was the business brains of the operation.

Like some of the Internet start-ups of today, the Disney brand was literally born in a garage, as Walt crafted his first cartoons in Kansas City, Missouri. In 1923, he moved to Los Angeles and opened the Disney Brothers Cartoon Studio. Its first works comprised a silent series called *Alice in Cartoonland*, which featured a little girl who entered an animated world. While certainly crude by today's standards, these films are still innovative and entertaining, displaying Walt's raw, non-stop creativity. But, by and large, during these years the name 'Disney' was indistinguishable from the other names that adorned the countless storefront studios that were strewn about Hollywood.

The transformation of Disney from a surname to a brand name took place in March 1928, thanks to a reversal that almost destroyed the company.

The Disney Brothers Cartoon Studio had achieved some success with a series based on a character called Oswald the Lucky Rabbit. But one day, in a meeting in New York, Walt found that the rights to Oswald had been taken away from him. On the train ride back to Los Angeles, determined to own the rights to anything he would ever create again, he sketched out a new character he called Mortimer Mouse. His wife, Lilian, looked at it and said she liked the drawing but hated the name. She insisted it be changed to Mickey. And so, a star was born.

Walt's recurrent inability to compromise creatively soon played a role in Mickey Mouse's debut. A cartoon short was produced starring Mickey, called *Plane Crazy*. But, before it was released, the first talking picture – *The Jazz Singer* – came out. Walt decided that Mickey's first cartoon would have sound, so he shelved *Plane Crazy* and produced *Steamboat Willie*. This was no small matter. Remember that the Disney Brothers Cartoon Studio was financially living a hand-to-mouth existence, so it was incredibly bold of Walt to keep this newly created asset on hold while he pushed ahead with new – and somewhat untested – technology.

His gamble paid off spectacularly. *Steamboat Willie* became an international success and Mickey Mouse and Walt Disney became household names.

If Walt Disney had only created Mickey Mouse, he would have been forever viewed as a giant in the entertainment industry. But Mickey was just the beginning. For three and a half decades, he continued to excel. Donald Duck, Goofy, Pluto, the Three Little Pigs, *Snow White and the Seven Dwarfs*, *Pinocchio* ... *Fantasia*, *Dumbo*, *Bambi*, *Cinderella* ... *Peter Pan*, *20,000 Leagues Under the Sea*, Disneyland Park, the Mickey Mouse Club, *Sleeping Beauty*, *101 Dalmatians*, *The Jungle Book*, *Mary Poppins*. This list is just the highest of the highlights. Walt kept breaking new ground until his death in 1966 when, until practically his last breath, he was working on the realization of his next dream: the development of 28,000 acres in central Florida that would be transformed into the Walt Disney World Resort. Thanks to Walt's unending flow of great product, 'Disney' came to be viewed by millions of people around the world as a safe haven – a name that could be trusted to provide quality, innovative entertainment for the entire family.

Obviously, I was around for none of this and can take no credit for the creation or development of the Disney brand. However, I take my responsibility as a steward of the brand very seriously: to protect it, enhance it and try to ensure that it is even more valuable and beloved in the twenty-first century than it was in the twentieth. It's a responsibility I share with all 120,000 Disney cast members around the world. We all know that the Disney brand is our most valuable asset. It is the sum total of our seventy-five years in business, of our reputation, of everything we stand for.

Improving a masterpiece

Upon arriving at Disney, the temptation was to view the Disney brand as one would a painting by Matisse and simply stand back and admire it. This was a temptation we had to resist because, unlike a work of art hanging on the wall of a museum, a brand is never a finished work. It is more like a pointillist painting on which innumerable new dots of colour are constantly being added, creating an ever-evolving image that is vital and meaningful to the public.

Enhancing a great brand while simultaneously retaining the attributes that are the source of its tremendous value can be a challenging balancing act. We've spent an enormous amount of time over the years experimenting, questioning and sometimes just outright anguishing over how to accomplish this task. As a result, we've developed a thorough understanding of our brand's fundamental characteristics and strengths. But it's not a science. The surest route to failure is to play it safe. We've learnt that, like our company's founder, we have to keep innovating. Some efforts are more successful than others are, but as long as we remain true to the core values of the brand, we have found that over the long-term we will achieve success. If we keep our palette fresh and vibrant, then dot by dot, the masterpiece that is the Disney brand will continue to enthral.

What we know about the Disney brand

We've always known that the Disney brand generates a level of loyalty and affection unlike any other brand. This deeply held affinity is obviously of great benefit to the company, but where does it come from? Why does it exist?

The answer is that Disney, unlike any other brand, is defined not just by its products, but also by deeply held emotions and values, such as family, fun, optimism and community. Think about it. There are many highly respected, very valuable brands, but their inherent value is derived *only* from a product or family of products. At Disney, great entertainment products have been (and always will be) the fundamental drivers of our success and are critical to our brand strength. However, our brand also derives a significant amount of its value from the personal beliefs and hopes that it evokes in people around the world.

Yes, parents take their children to the Walt Disney World Resort or to a Disney animated feature film because they know they can expect innovative, top-quality family entertainment. However, parents are also likely to associate the Disney brand with more deeply rooted attitudes and expectations, such as the importance of spending time together as a family, and the joy of watching their children at play. These associations are personal and universal (what parent doesn't enjoy the sound of a child's laughter?) and they are among the reasons people establish such deep bonds with our brand.

As Disney's chairman and CEO, I am thrilled that our brand offers such a unique advantage that no competitor could replicate it. But, as the person ultimately responsible for this amazing asset, I am also awed by the emotional investment our guests make in the brand, and not a little bit humbled by the fact that Walt and Roy were able to create something that offers a seemingly endless supply of enjoyment and fun for all people.

This leads me to another fundamental characteristic of the Disney brand: people pass their love for Disney to their children, who in turn instil it in their children. Thus, brand loyalty is passed uninterrupted and undiminished from one generation to the next. This too is wonderful for the company, but why does it happen? Again, it goes back to the fact that the Disney brand represents not just products, but also an emotional touchstone that is universal and timeless. The children who paid a nickel for a movie ticket and laughed at the antics of Mickey and Donald grew up and had children who plopped down in front of a black-and-white television set every afternoon to watch *The Mickey Mouse Club*. They grew up and had children, who now spend their afternoons playing interactive games at the Disney.com site on the Internet. And all three generations attend the Sunday matinee performance of *The Lion King* on Broadway.

Obviously the Disney entertainment experience has changed a great deal during these three generations due to technological innovations and our expansion into new markets. But the reason people seek out and enjoy Disney entertainment remains virtually unchanged: Disney offers a way for families to share a great entertainment experience. Thus, families pass the Disney tradition from one generation of children to the next.

What is the source of the 'Disney magic'?

It is true that no customer wants to hear that his new car has 'magic brakes', or that his new computer contains a 'magical hard drive'. However, the Disney magic is indeed what has drawn people to the company for nearly eighty years; it is the summation of everything they expect from the brand. But where does magic come from? What does it look like? The answer to those questions can be found in the faces of the more than 120,000 Disney cast members around the world. They are the source of the Disney magic, and one of the most important aspects of my job is to maintain an environment that enables our cast members to perform their magic for our guests.

Specifically, that includes communicating the very high performance standards that all cast members – from executive staff to part-time workers – are expected to meet. Our guests associate the Disney brand with an experience that is meaningful, happy and magical, and thus their expectations of Disney are incredibly high. Our cast members understand that they must not only meet those expectations; they must exceed them. That's why cast members in every Disney business perform their jobs with a degree of professionalism, commitment and zeal that simply isn't found anywhere else.

Magic is in the details

The philosophy that Walt and Roy instilled in the corporate culture – and that I try to perpetuate – is that magic flows from the details. We know that it's often the smallest, simplest details that make the greatest impression on people. We also know that you can never tell exactly which details will make a difference to your audience. So we try not to neglect any.

One example is the animated feature film, *The Lion King*. If you have children, I'm sure you've at least seen the video – again and again and again. But, even so, there just may be a few details of this film that have escaped your attention. For example, there is a scene in which the elephants are walking across the plain, leaving a wake of dust in their path. It's not a major scene and if you were to view it you might think, 'So what's the big deal? Elephants are big. The Serengeti is dusty. Dust happens.' True. But have you ever tried to draw dust? Much less animate it? It would have taken years to move around the tens of thousands of tiny specks in that scene. And since we didn't have years, we spent weeks devising a computer animation program that could create convincing dust. I don't recall any movie reviewers who praised the quality of this particular effect, and there is no Academy Award for 'Best Dust in an Animated Feature', but without the small details like this one, it just wouldn't be the same film. And, more importantly, it wouldn't have the magic that our audience expects of a Disney film.

Disney is teeming with people whose job it is to ensure that our guests experience that magic every time they interact with our company. Whether it's the grand gestures, such as the jaw-dropping animal parade sequence that opens the stage production of *The Lion King*, or the mundane act of steam cleaning the grounds of our theme parks every night after the gates close, our cast members give it their absolute best effort – the secret ingredient of magic.

Magic as a corporate strategy

As chairman and CEO, my job is to provide a corporate structure and culture that enables our imagineers, animators and other cast members to perform their creative and technical feats, and also perpetuate the values and traditions that fuel the Disney magic – and thus the value of our brand. I am, in effect, the chief brand manager, and my responsibilities include both the pragmatic and the inspirational.

For example, I strongly believe that everyone at Disney must understand our brand philosophy, and how to incorporate it into their job. That's one reason I instituted 'Disney Dimensions', a nine-day immersion in Disney culture in which groups of senior Disney executives spend almost every waking hour learning every aspect of the company. It is – by design – a kind of Hell Week at the happiest place on Earth, and I know that the executives who complete (I'm sure some would use the word 'endure') the pro-grammes have a much deeper understanding of the company and the brand.

Programmes begin each day at 7 a.m. and end no earlier than 10 p.m. Executives in charge of each of our five business units provide detailed presentations about their respective businesses.

Participants are also immersed in hands-on experiences. For example, they don't just tour a theme park; they don character costumes and interact with guests, performing the job just as a typical cast member would. At first, they usually feel awkward and uncomfortable – wearing a Pluto costume in the Florida heat and humidity can be a bit stifling. But their attitudes quickly change once they see the first smile on a child's face. They just want to be the best Pluto they can be, and make damn sure that the next child's smile is even bigger. They become part of the Disney magic.

Lessons in the values, traditions and expectations of the Disney brand are not limited to senior management. In fact, all Disney cast members participate in a brand stewardship programme as part of their training at the Disney University when they join the company. Although the programme is tailored to specific Disney businesses, all new cast members learn about the brand's history and its core principles and values on their very first day as a Disney employee.

One of the roles I literally play on behalf of the Disney brand is as host of the Sunday night *Wonderful World of Disney* television show on ABC. Anyone who has ever seen it understands that I'm not a born thespian. But, these brief stints before the camera have, I believe, achieved two valuable things: they have helped to add a human face to the Disney company and they have certainly given me a greater appreciation of actors! It's another dot on the canvas of the Disney brand.

Synergy

Another initiative we have instituted is the formalization of synergy within the company, making it a core corporate function for expanding and enhancing the brand. We probably have the only senior vice president of synergy in the world, who oversees a myriad of company-wide initiatives, ranging from the launch of a film like *Dinosaur* to the optimization of a TV hit like *Who Wants To Be a Millionaire* to the millennium celebration at the Walt Disney World Resort. Our synergy group coordinates and leverages the contributions of our various business units for each initiative, thus creating a multiplier effect for the individual project and the overall Disney brand that could not be accomplished otherwise.

Brand management

We also created a formal brand management structure that includes a system of policies and review procedures to ensure that the integrity and value of the brand is never diminished. True, this aspect of the Disney brand story sounds less than magical, but it is our insistence on maintaining very high standards and our steadfast resistance to compromising the integrity of our brand that enables Disney to consistently meet the great expectations of our guests.

For example, the brand management team is responsible for reviewing virtually all marketing and advertising material to ensure that the Disney brand is represented in an appropriate manner. If we are launching a new Walt Disney Pictures film, the team will scrutinize virtually every aspect of the publicity campaign, including television ads, signage and toys. They're looking for anything the public might consider inappropriate or which conflicts with the principles of the Disney brand. And if they find it, the material is reworked.

The brand management team has also established strict rules designed to retain the integrity of the brand. You won't find Mickey,

Goofy, Winnie the Pooh or any other beloved Disney icon stepping out of character into the role of salesperson for any product – and this includes Disney products. We do allow our characters to appear in advertising that showcases Disney entertainment. For example, through our partnership with the McDonald's Corporation, we showcase our characters in a way that increases public interest in the films and videos in which they appear. However, our characters do not directly promote McDonald's products.

There's no doubt that a character such as Mickey, who has been the Disney icon for decades and who is recognized and beloved around the world, could sell a lot of sneakers and toothpaste, and provide our company with a tidy profit in the process. However, the reason for Mickey's enduring popularity is the fact that people feel they know him. He is fun and lovable and optimistic and he adores children. People understand that when they see Mickey, they will get a smile, a wave and a great big hug. Those aspects of Mickey are as enduring and as reliable as the sun. To alter the relationship that our guests have with Mickey or any of his friends might provide our company with short-term profits, but would ultimately diminish the special bond they share and thus harm the Disney brand.

In fact, our brand management group spends a great deal of time balancing the requirement of near-term profits with the need to preserve the long-term value of the brand. The fact is that Disney is a publicly held company, with a duty to manage its businesses in a way that enhances shareholder value. That could potentially create the temptation to leverage our most valuable asset – the Disney brand – to improve our performance *today*. Luckily, our brand management team and our senior executives understand that the brand must be viewed not as an asset for just this quarter or this year, but for this century and beyond. And business decisions regarding the brand are made with that philosophy in mind.

For example, many financial institutions would pay us handsomely to market their products and services to children. However, we believe such a relationship would be an inappropriate use of our brand. Financial products and services are not complementary to Disney's family entertainment businesses, and linking them could create two problems: the core values that people associate with the Disney brand, such as fun and family, could get diluted. Even worse, we could damage the bond of trust we have with parents who might believe we are taking advantage of children's love for Disney in order to directly sell them 'grown-up' products that should be purchased under a parent's watchful eye.

Know your brand

As I mentioned earlier, a great brand evolves and changes – and thus so does the public's relationship with it. That's why one of the most important responsibilities of our brand management team is to study the strength of the Disney brand across various markets, geographic locations and demographic groups. They are continuously evaluating specific criteria such as brand awareness and consumer perception and then reporting those results to my senior management team and me. If we discover that people's attitudes toward the brand have become less favourable in a certain country, we find the source of the problem and then implement strategies to restore and improve brand affiliation in that region.

For example, one study by our brand management group revealed that awareness of Disney in one country was very high. In fact, it was too high. The public were beginning to feel that Disney was 'everywhere' and thus their attitude towards our company was becoming increasingly negative. Over exposure was threatening the integrity of the brand.

The source of the problem became apparent once we reviewed the data. We had been implementing high-profile, broad-based marketing programmes for a myriad of products, including films, new theme parks and attractions and licensed merchandise. Unfortunately, the strategy had created a fairly serious problem: consumers were confronted with so many Disney messages they weren't focusing on any one of them, and thus our efforts were largely being wasted. Even worse, people were becoming a tad resentful, feeling they couldn't turn the corner without seeing or hearing about Disney. Instead of creating a symphony with our various campaigns, we had created a cacophony. And the public was covering its ears.

The solution, of course, was to lower the volume. We shifted from a mass marketing approach to a more targeted strategy. We eliminated several initiatives, and those we kept were scaled back and reworked to target smaller but more specific audiences that were more likely to be receptive to the message.

The plan worked. By using a more focused marketing strategy, we were able to attract the consumers most likely to purchase certain products without distracting – or annoying – them with information about other Disney products in which they had less interest. A follow-up study showed that the strategy worked: perceptions of excessive commercialism changed, and the public's positive attitude towards our brand returned.

This episode taught us a valuable lesson: while you can never make too many great products, you can promote them too aggress-ively, and you can cross the line between enhancing brand awareness and giving the appearance of exploiting the brand. As a result, while we continue to work hard to introduce the Disney brand to new markets and new regions of the world, we evaluate the methods for doing so very carefully.

Brand and the bottom line

I've talked a lot about the value of the Disney brand and the effort we put into preserving and enhancing its value. At this point, you may be wondering whether 'value' refers to nothing more than the intrinsic worth the brand has to the Walt Disney Company. It is true that those of us who work at Disney value the brand because it represents our corporate heritage and our reputation. However, when we say that the brand is our most valuable asset, we mean it in the most literal sense. Without a doubt, the brand is far more valuable – in a real-world, dollars-and-cents way – than any other asset Disney owns.

During the last fifteen years, Disney's market capitalization has grown from $3 billion to approximately $80 billion. Revenues have grown from $2 billion to more than $25 billion. It's no coincidence that this incredible growth occurred as we undertook an unprecedented effort to expand the brand into new markets and new regions. Clearly, the brand is a critical source of strategic strength and an important contributor to the bottom-line profit of all our businesses.

Consider the brand's financial impact on our film business. Study after study shows that a movie with the Walt Disney Studios label will generate greater revenues *than if exactly the same film* were labelled with the name of another studio. Why? Because the public associates the Disney brand with the highest-quality family entertainment and thus chooses it above other brands. In effect, the brand guarantees higher profits.

The brand also lowers the barriers of entry when Disney decides to expand into new markets – something we've done many times during my tenure as chairman and CEO. The brand provides an inherent level of public awareness and a build-in customer base, which in turn lowers the amount of capital we need to invest in a new venture, and increases our probability of success.

For example, in 1993, we decided to enter the cruise line business, believing that a cruise line catering to families was a natural fit with our theme parks and resorts business. We knew it wouldn't be easy. After all, the business has several well-established, well-known competitors. Also, while our seven theme parks and approximately thirty hotels make us a leader in the travel and recreation business, we had no direct experience in the cruise line business. And building, staffing and managing an 83,000-ton ship is not an easy – or inexpensive – undertaking. However, as we studied the business and developed our strategy, it became obvious that the brand would provide us with some important advantages that would make the initiative not just feasible, but would give us a high probability of success.

In this case, the public was aware that cruise ships were an entirely new venture for us, but they also knew from experience that they could expect an unparalleled level of imagination, quality and attention to detail – in short, a generous dose of magic – from the Disney Cruise Line. The public trusted the Disney brand, a fact demonstrated quite clearly by the fact that when our new cruise ship – named, appropriately, *Disney Magic* – launched from Port Canaveral, Florida in July 1998, it was almost fully booked for the rest of the year.

We launched our second ship, *Disney Wonder*, in 1999. In typical Disney fashion, we had spent the preceding year making a thousand changes and improvements to the ships and the overall business and most importantly had demonstrated to our guests that their trust in our brand had not been misplaced. The Disney Cruise Line offered an exceptional and unique family vacation experience that certainly reflected our guests' high expectations and upheld the legacy of the brand.

A year later as I write this, the Disney Cruise Line continues to exceed our performance expectations. I don't think any other company could have achieved such levels of performance in such a short time without the kind of built-in performance boost provided by the Disney brand.

Consumers' strong affiliation with the Disney brand also means that they are likely to be customers of more than one Disney business. The family that visits Disneyland, for example, probably loves Disney-branded films, and shops at the Disney Store, generating a kind of 'brand driven' revenue stream for our company.

In fact, brand affinity is so strong among such a large group of our customers that this year we are establishing a new programme that will enable us to identify and communicate with them. This Internet-based initiative will allow us to develop a more personalized relationship with our most avid customers, providing special offers, discounts and events and it will, hopefully, allow us to further expand the interaction our customers have with our various products and businesses.

Our international business also receives a strong bottom-line boost from our brand. As I mentioned previously, people around the world trust the Disney brand because it represents the best entertainment products available *and* it evokes personal beliefs and values. Also because people personalize the brand in this way, they don't necessarily view Disney as 'American'. Instead, they incorporate Disney characters and products into their own cultures, which ultimately makes it easier for us to expand the brand into new regions, and to cultivate deep, long-term brand loyalty.

Consider our experience in Italy. In the 1930s, Disney started publishing a Mickey Mouse comic book there, where Mickey was not known by his American name. Instead he was dubbed Topolino, and he became a beloved figure in that country. Thanks to Topolino's popularity, our publishing business thrived in Italy, and enabled us to introduce a wide range of Disney products into the Italian market. Today, Topolino is as beloved as he was sixty-five years ago, and Italy is one of Disney's strongest markets outside the US.

Our theme parks in particular are important 'tentpoles' for establishing the brand outside the US. For example, the opening of the Tokyo Disneyland Park in 1983 sharply increased the brand's profile in Japan, enabling us to significantly expand our presence in that market. The brand has grown so strong there that next year we will open an entirely new theme park, called Tokyo DisneySea, adjacent to Tokyo Disneyland, and this, we hope, will start the process all over again.

In 1993 we opened our sixth theme park, Euro Disney just outside Paris. And although this theme park, now called Disneyland Paris Resort, struggled financially in its early years, it was the most popular paid tourist destination in Europe from the day it opened, and is now profitable. Meanwhile, sales of Disney products in Europe have increased by ten times from two years before Disneyland Paris opened until five years after. In 2002, Disneyland Paris will be joined by a second theme park, and we expect the magic of Disney synergy to strengthen the brand and all its benefits even more.

Upholding the brand legacy

I am still awed by the two young men who by virtue of determination, talent and a deep love for their craft and the public created this extraordinary entity we call the Disney brand. Since then, generations of people around the world have embraced Disney and all that it stands for.

It's quite a legacy to uphold. As head of the Walt Disney Company, I work hard to ensure that the brand remains relevant and meaningful to our fans and guests. I know this deeply held sense of responsibility is shared by all Disney cast members. We understand that people will always have high expectations for their 'Disney experience'. They will hold us to a higher standard because that is the implicit promise of the brand.

And that's great because it creates a kind of 'circle of expectations': we at Disney continuously try to improve upon an already high performance standard, and in the process we burnish that amazing and unique entity called the Disney brand. In doing so, we provide even greater enjoyment for guests, which, I like to think, would make Walt and Roy pretty happy as well.

Commentary

Great brands stand the test of time and Disney is the most wonderful cross-generational brand, as Michael Eisner has shown. How many other brands can relate so powerfully to children, parents, grand-parents and even great grand-parents?

But great brands need great brand management. It is clear from every anecdote that Walt Disney himself was an instinctive brand manager, like so many entrepreneurs. Disney, now, needs a different style in order to manage its complexity and maximize the synergy from its component parts.

The importance of the organizational structure and culture to the delivery of the Disney brand cannot be emphasized enough.

Anyone who has been to a Disney resort can testify to the quality of every individual who works there and to the management of the experience. Every member of the cast is trained, with the clear recognition that those who sweep the immaculate streets are the most likely to be asked for directions.

The old adage that 'the devil is in the detail' is to me certainly true in the delivery of service brands. You just have to have a system of training and managing your people to deliver your brand how you want it. It is significant that Michael clearly wants to be identified as brand manager-in-chief. How many other chief executives accept what that role entails?

3 | INSEAD: Management Education with a Mission

GABRIEL HAWAWINI, *dean*

INSEAD as an institution celebrated its fortieth anniversary in 1999. INSEAD the brand is much younger, only being adopted as the name of the business school in the early 1990s. By comparison with its major competitors such as Harvard or Wharton, INSEAD is a very young institution and even younger brand. The dean of INSEAD, Gabriel Hawawini, explains how INSEAD became such a distinctive brand and its exciting plans for the future.

INSEAD's brand resides in the story of how a small educational start-up in Europe exploded into one of the world's largest and most successful business schools – without really (until quite recently) managing its brand at all. What it has managed – and expanded with unremitting passion and creativity – is its mission.

Since its founding, at the birth of the European Community some forty years ago, INSEAD sought to rise above national boundaries, to bring talented individuals and businesses together in a safe 'haven' of exchange and learning, without dominant cultural or ideological paradigms. This mission was needed in the Europe of 1959 and it is increasingly relevant to the debate that accompanies the globalization of the world's economy, especially in the new economies of Asia.

Time has crafted INSEAD's brand. Today, our brand stands for the accomplishments of forty years' worth of efforts, and is not the result of professional spending on marketing strategies. Indeed, we now recognize that it is high time that we harnessed the power of our brand, to further the breadth and depth of INSEAD's message and mission.

Europe unites

What sounds obvious today was far from clear in the Europe of 1959, still licking its wartime wounds, still profoundly divided by culture, language and history. In its genesis as the Institut Européen d'Administration des Affaires, INSEAD was first imagined by a Frenchman, General Georges F. Doriot, who had emigrated to the US and become a renowned Harvard Business School professor. With one foot well grounded on each of two continents, he sought to introduce some American ideas on business school education, based on the pragmatic application of real-life examples and in-company project work, to the more theoretical approaches dear to European universities at the time. From the international perspective born of emigration, he saw it as a European project, not a national one – in the days before 'Europe' had itself become a reality.

It was a very early application of what would become the school's longstanding tradition of mixing, matching and disseminating best practices from one company to another, from one country to another, from one region of the world to another. Doriot was both the inspiration and archetype. INSEAD alumni around the world are ambassadors of his vision and apt reflections of his dream – cosmopolitan business people with one foot in different realities, comfortable with cultural contradictions and paradox, and active believers in business and entrepreneurship as agents of economic development and wealth creation.

Partnering with business

An essential ingredient to the success of this mission was INSEAD's closeness to business. The school was created and supported by companies and business leaders. It has stayed very close to their preoccupations ever since. Unlike most of the world's other leading business schools, it is completely independent. It has no links to any university, government, or other organization of any kind. We know very clearly who our customers are, and our financial viability over the years has depended on responding effectively to their preoccupations and guaranteeing them access to outstanding research and ideas from a world-class faculty.

The structure of the school's governing bodies reflects its constant preoccupation with nurturing these relationships and understanding the needs of business. The school's International Council meets once a year and is chaired by global business leaders. It also has a network of National Councils in each country made up of national business leaders. The dialogue is constant, influential and strategic. Few other educational institutions listen as closely and as constantly to their constituencies.

The appreciation seems to be mutual. Few other business schools raise as much funding from the corporate sector as INSEAD does. In its recent fundraising campaign (1996–2000), 80 per cent of the funds raised came from corporate donations. Business – especially international business – has come to trust the INSEAD brand. Companies tend to work with the school across several dimensions: partnering with the school to fund research, recruiting its MBA graduates as proven sources of high-potential international managers, and sending their own executives for regular doses of lifelong learning. A virtuous, repetitive cycle keeps companies linked into the brand at various and regular stages of their development.

Delivering the brand

The umbrella INSEAD brand covers several different 'service' areas that operate as different departments within the organization:

- **MBA Programme**: one of the world's largest MBA programmes and a precursor of the 'more experienced student' model. Participants are on average twenty-eight years old and have five years of professional experience. Over 700 MBA students graduate each year – and over 125 companies come on-site to recruit them. The extremely stringent admissions process, complete with two personal interviews of candidates by alumni, and the more than 3,500 applications received each year, guarantee an exceptional level of quality. The intensity of the one-year programme, the quality of participants and the faculty research that infuses the teaching curriculum combine into a memorable, often life-changing, year. In 2000, INSEAD was rated the number one international MBA by both the *Financial Times* and *Business Week*'s annual rankings.

– **Executive Education**: INSEAD also runs one of the world's largest executive education programmes, attracting more than 6,000 participants each year. Many of these are involved in company-specific courses specifically tailored in terms of research, content and even delivery to a given company's issues and needs. We were among the first business schools in the world to offer such a degree of corporate learning customization. This flexibility and willingness to both adapt and innovate has proven to be a vital competitive advantage and INSEAD routinely features among the world's top-ranked executive education institutions.

– **Research and Development**: 140 full-time faculty staff from twenty-six different countries fuel INSEAD's growing academic influence. Over the years, research relevance and rigour has become the school's primary focus, recognized as a key factor of its long-term success. A demanding but also highly entrepreneurial R & D culture strongly supports innovation and original approaches.

– **PhD Programme**: In 1988, to extend the influence and reach of its intellectual influence and brand, INSEAD decided to create its own PhD programme. A four-year residential doctoral programme, its success has been measured by the quality of positions offered to its graduates, now teaching at some of the world's most prestigious business schools, including Harvard, Stanford and Chicago in the US, Keio

University in Japan and LBS and IMD in Europe. In 2001, there were fifty-two students pursuing PhDs at INSEAD.

Multiculturalism as mantra

Certainly the most dominant and defining characteristic of INSEAD's brand is its internationalism. Although every business school on earth now boasts this adjective, few can claim to have their foundations resting in its very definition. INSEAD was created to be international, to span cultures, to build bridges. The definition of the word has never stopped expanding since, but the openness and non-judgmental curiosity that informed INSEAD's origins remain almost evangelically intact. The school's slogan, '*enrichment through diversity*', is a deeply held belief, and informs the institution's recruiting, selection processes, research agenda, teaching approaches and student body.

The more than 700 MBAs in the programme represent fifty-eight different nationalities. Each individual, on average, speaks at least three languages and half have worked outside their home countries. No single nationality represents more than 10 per cent of the student body. The number of Latin American, Eastern European and Asian students has risen dramatically over the past decade as these regions have evolved and developed economically. Today, INSEAD's face – and brand – reflect the globalization of the business world itself.

Diversity is seen not as an issue to be managed, but as a source of new ideas, new responses and intellectual breakthroughs. The definition of the word goes well beyond a collection of nationalities, always an integral part of the school's profile. It includes openness to other perspectives, other research approaches, other teaching methods and opinions than one's own. We recognize, however, that even our own rather broad definition of 'diversity' needs to expand even further, and to answer even more comprehensively the global challenges of race, gender and equality of access.

Our lack of national affiliation has given INSEAD a unique image, one that sits unrivalled (and rather alone) in the world today.

It may also be one of the reasons that INSEAD had some trouble imposing its brand in its early days – there was no single market, no obvious competitor, no existing benchmark. Not even the brand name itself was obvious. For its first three decades, INSEAD was officially called the **Institute Européen d'Ad**ministration des Affaires. Later, it was often amicably referred to as just 'Fontainebleau'. Only in the early 1990s did we work with professional corporate image consultants to assist us in repositioning and labelling the brand to be more in line with our ambitions and our dominantly non-francophone audience. We then officially switched to using the acronym that had by then become the way our friends, customers and alumni referred to us – INSEAD.

Today, business and markets have, in a sense, caught up with the thinking behind our model. Business is now convinced of the astuteness and relevance of INSEAD's global mindset, which in turn add strength and credence to its brand, and has become a profound competitive barrier. INSEAD's diversity has been recognized as a source of the most astounding enrichment to all who have experienced it. That realization – often experienced as a personal epiphany – intimately informs our brand and the experiences associated with all its activities. It also explains why, without huge expenditures in marketing, INSEAD has become a globally recognized name. There is no other place on the planet quite like it.

International networks

Probably the most potent vector of INSEAD's brand is its alumni network. Most alumni readily admit that their time in a forest in Fontainebleau changed their lives. Shocked, inspired and challenged by their classmates and professors, participants leave each year with widened perspectives and global networks. When alumni graduate from INSEAD's MBA or executive programmes, they find that their enjoyment of the multicultural microcosm brought to life in a pretty campus just outside Paris (and now in a pretty campus in central Singapore as well) often results in their having more in common with other INSEAD alumni than with their own countrymen. They have, for a year, rubbed shoulders with people and ideas from all over the world. This heady perspective is addictive and makes INSEAD's alumni networks particularly tightly knit, and a record 60 per cent of alumni (compared to other leading business schools) remain paid-up members of their alumni association.

The strength of the experience also ensures an unusually tenacious personal and emotional attachment to the brand and its associated memories. At alumni reunions, organized five, ten, twenty, thirty and even forty years after graduation, a record percentage of each year group returns to the campus to rekindle connections and networks.

Some 20,000 people strong, the official alumni network is represented by thirty-six active national alumni associations around the globe. Connected by regular events in many of the world's capitals, and by a growing presence on the institution's website (which has more than 4 million hits each month), the alumni themselves are a large part of the strength of INSEAD's brand. Alumni are present in every geographical area, in every sector, in every leading company, and are usually in highly visible executive positions. They *are*, in many respects, the brand. When people see alumni, they see the brand brought to life. Few brands can boast such able, loyal and eloquent emissaries.

Asia restructures

In 1997, we concluded that what INSEAD had managed in Europe was much needed in Asia. After two decades developing research and teaching in Asia via a dedicated Euro-Asia Centre, INSEAD decided that the Asian region needed an on-site, world-class supplier of management education and that global businesses needed more in-depth research and assistance across ever broader market horizons. There was much to learn from Asia . . . and Asia had much to learn from the rest of the world.

Our Singapore campus is the greatest opportunity that INSEAD has ever had. It allows us to question – and redefine – the model of the business school itself. At the dawn of a new century, we need to ask if the current model of the business school, created in the US at the beginning of the last century, is still relevant to the world in which we live today.

Assuming stature

It is a bold move. It was a huge gamble and a huge investment made with incredible – some said impossible – time pressures. But it is perfectly in line with INSEAD's founding focus and philosophy. That professionally educated business managers and respected, independent research would be a positive force in developing healthy and competitive markets and societies. Not unlike the Europe of 1959, the Asia of 1999 needed to think regionally and globally and set aside its national rivalries and limited horizons. And, in the aftermath of the Asian crisis, there was a widespread realization that the time had come for business leaders, politicians and other change agents to come together to prepare the future.

INSEAD is different from any other business school. In Singapore, we are not talking about creating a system to disseminate the ideas and knowledge developed in a core location (as all the other business schools are doing). Nor are we talking about creating a research and teaching institution dedicated to Asia, which we have done for the past twenty years with the Euro-Asia Centre. Rather, we are experimenting with creating the world's first *globally connected* business school. INSEAD will be an institution with campuses of equal weight researching and teaching global business issues in each of the world's primary economic regions, enriched by the varied perspectives of each region's culture and environment.

If we only create Asia's most successful business school, we will not have accomplished our mission. Instead, we imagine a series of connected campuses where people and ideas circulate freely – and constantly. A minority of the MBA students in Singapore (and a growing proportion of the MBAs in Fontainebleau) are actually from Asia. This proves that INSEAD continues doing in Asia what it has done for the past forty years in Fontainebleau – developing truly global leaders and research with no dominant cultural paradigm.

Going for global

So the INSEAD brand is expanding its geographical breadth, but not really its meaning or approach. The most international of schools has simply become *more* international. The brand's characteristics may largely explain the immediate success of the Singapore campus. INSEAD was already international; it had already integrated lessons and networks from Asia, and it had already carried out decades of research there. Classes are full. Students are enthusiastically splitting their MBA year between continents. Executive courses that span the two campuses are in demand by global clients who have long wanted business schools to reflect their own global structures. And faculty staff are settling in Asia, excited by the chance to lead innovation on the frontiers of research and education.

Timing and context also shaped the move. Competitive pressures were rising. Leading American business schools were studying and opening satellite operations and joint ventures in Asia. The business school game was increasingly evolving into a two-tiered playing field – the global players versus the local or regional players. With our Asian expansion, we have made a clear jump into the first league.

Strengthening differentiation

We are the only business school in the world with the guts to put resident faculty staff on a true second campus. A school is really about people. It is the students and lecturers and researchers that make it happen. In September 2001, INSEAD had more than twenty staff residents in Singapore, and we plan to grow that to forty over the next four years. We are not there to disseminate ideas developed in Fontainebleau. We would like to learn from and listen to what is happening in Asia and thereby improve our understanding of global business everywhere.

Globalization debated

A force for good

We believe that business – and therefore business schools – have a growing role to play in a world that is ever more global and ever more connected: where the flow of people, goods and ideas has proven to be a source of unprecedented growth and economic development. Globalization is celebrated by many, but it is also feared by a growing and increasingly vocal minority. Born and bred as a non-national school, INSEAD's duty is to do more than respond to the expanding needs of its global corporate clients. We must play a major role in this wider debate. How? By researching the advantages and disadvantages of globalization, by de-politicising the debate around it, and by bringing the different voices together into a constructive dialogue in a neutral environment.

Each phase of development is a logical extension of the vision that created INSEAD. That vision goes beyond simply educating the next generation's business leaders. We see our role as helping international business to promote the wealth, openness and exchange that have proven to be the foundation of the world's development. This was why INSEAD was established in post-war Europe. Singapore represents the first extension of this vision onto the global stage.

From nodes to webs

But Singapore is a launch pad. Once we prove our model's effectiveness across two campuses and test it successfully in Asia, we will have earned the right to roll it out to the world's other key global markets. After Europe and Asia, North America would be the logical next step. We can then describe our current configuration as the first two nodes of a global knowledge web.

Students, faculty staff, ideas and experience will be encouraged to flow seamlessly between the nodes, and to build strong, lifelong relationships throughout the web. The power of this kind of network, at this quality level, will be immense.

INSEAD to the power^e

The success of this vision depends, like all visions, on its implementation. In our case, much hinges on leveraging the promises and potential of technology. E-learning will be the lynchpin that allows our global vision to come alive. Knowledge will be its lifeblood, education its means of transmission and networking its claim to sustainability. Our second campus in Singapore gives us the chance to test, refine and perfect e-learning technologies and applications. It gives our faculty a vast terrain of research and experimentation. If our nodal network structure proves effective between Europe and Asia, we will work on extending it to the world's major markets.

In our brand lies our founding dream: to look beyond the world's many divisions for its commonalities, to harness the best ideas and energies that the world has to offer, and to create knowledge networks that will actively teach and influence the world in the future. In that vision lies our opportunities. We aren't here to manage our brand. We're here to help global business and business leaders create the wealth and exchange that underpin the world's development. Our brand will symbolize tomorrow, as it does today, the success of our mission.

Commentary

INSEAD is a good example of a brand which has emerged rather than been designed. No one set out to create the most distinctive brand in the increasingly crowded world marketplace for business education. But those who founded and developed INSEAD did create a very distinctive set of cultural and professional values which were easily understood, by those who deliver them as well as those who are 'customers'. Like so many professional organizations INSEAD relies for delivery of its brand proposition and brand values on a number of individual professionals. These cultural values were assimilated by all those who worked at INSEAD, and indeed influenced the selection process. It is therefore not surprising that, over time, these values began to create a true brand, because they were both distinctive and aspirational.

It is interesting to note that now INSEAD has recognized the value of the brand and as it expands geographically it will need to manage the branding process more carefully and systematize the transmission of cultural values, rather than rely on the informality and geographical unity of the past.

4 | Psion: The Battle for Wire-free Working

DAVID POTTER, *founder and chairman*

Positioned at the intersection of telephone and computer technology, Psion is preparing to launch Net-ready mobiles. As part of a powerful global alliance ranged against Microsoft, Psion is no ordinary company. Its founder, chairman and CEO David Potter, explains how he has become King of the 'hand-helds' and is aiming to keep things that way.

Making sense of the wizardry

Psion was set up in 1980 as an innovation company and now participates in and leads segments of the giant revolution that is underway in the world which, in my view, will prove to be of greater significance than the industrial revolution and the steam engine.

At Psion we are not interested in innovation for its own sake, however, but see it as a means to deliver greater benefit and utility. We are interested in the way people live. We are looking to change things for them – to help and participate in their lives. We *root* creativity, using it to ask the fundamental question – how is this going to benefit our customers in new and better ways? – not as a measure of what others are doing. Creation of the invention is one thing, but it is equally difficult to harness that customer benefit – which is what we focus on at Psion.

Our roots are innovation and software. The public perception of Psion is the personal organizer product, which became a powerful eighties symbol. For the investment community, our business clients and our partners, Psion has a far bigger offer: we are now a group of companies focused on emerging mobile Internet markets – powerfully placed to contribute to (and profit from) the new economy. Our brand values seem to be consistent across all our audiences.

Innovation is the strongest brand value – an ability to look into the future and to harness the emerging technologies. Our approach to innovation is to take the technology, a market overview and an understanding of what the customer would like to be able to do and put them together to provide breakthrough solutions. Innovation is a state of mind. There's an open-minded way of taking in stimulus here. What can't people do that they'd like to do?

The organizer is an ideal example of what I mean. When we developed our first hand-held computer notebook at the beginning of the eighties, laptops did not exist. We were in a café in Maida Vale and got round to the subject of so-called 'personal' computers. I remember we drew a picture on a napkin of a table with a machine on top and lots of little blue footsteps going to and from it to indicate that this wasn't a *personal* computer at all. At the time computers were so big and expensive they tended to be used by several people, rather like an office photocopier. The question was how could one produce a device, at much lower cost, that would genuinely be used by the individual. Such a concept implied mobility, so we then got the idea of a highly portable or ubiquitous computer as we called it. From the napkin to production took two years. It was a radical concept. There were calculators on the market but we had the idea of information management and created the word 'organizer' to describe it. We also invented the first solid-state disk, which was the core point of making a useful computer that would retain information when you switched off the power.

The Psion Organizer was originally targeted at consumers but it also proved enormously useful to industry and commerce – with a seemingly infinite wealth of applications. Our own programme language, with which sector specialist software writers happily wrote, enabled easy, rapid universal tailoring of the organizer. Psion devices and technology were everywhere – in supermarkets, factories, farms, airports . . . the list is endless.

Our newest product, Wavefinder, demonstrates the consistency of our approach and values. Wavefinder is a digital radio of the type that broadcasters have long been promising, but we are the first to produce a suitable set. Typical of the Psion approach and philosophy, Wavefinder has turned radio from a passive to an active medium allowing you perfect recording, time-shifting (so you listen when you want to, not just when transmitted), and wire-free access website to website. It even allows you to see the radio broadcasting. It plugs into your desktop computer with a quirky etiolated pale-blue body and a cyclops-like, pulsating, multi-coloured light. Like the organizer and our earliest software products, Wavefinder has that magic ingredient of making you want something you didn't realize you wanted.

The organic route to growth

At Psion we have a history of consistent organic growth. There is no single niche or activity which could therefore be said to define us, although from the beginning we've been in innovative software.

Along the way, over the past twenty years, we've been active in five different important niches. We started in the software games market and were number one in innovative software. Next there was the Organizer; then the Organizer Series 3, with its sixteen-bit technology – when we leapt ahead of the Japanese and Hewlett-Packard in terms of vision and aspiration. This led to the dense PC card modems in which we were number one in Europe and number two or three worldwide. This in turn led onto our forming Symbian with Nokia, Ericsson, Motorola and Matsushita with technology to bring the wireless environment to fruition. Key to each phase in our transition has been our software, which has always been very innovative, user-friendly and robust, far away from the c:/ prompt and complicated codes that had been the norm.

Thus the essence of Psion is one entity – Symbian, Psion Computers and Psion Teklogix all go back to 1984 (the roots of Symbian go back to the beginning of the company in 1981). Dacom (now

Psion Connect) was acquired in 1988–9. We realized in the eighties that mobile computing on the one hand and communications on the other were like apple pie and cream – they have to go together. We bought Dacom to provide that communications expertise and the development of the PC card came directly from that. Importantly Dacom provided communications skills to the rest of the group.

In 1996, we restructured Psion into four companies. This was partly to have a flatter structure and to provide more autonomy and independence and drive to each of these individual sectors. This structure is necessary to foster the independence of spirit which provides the atmosphere in which innovation can flourish. Psion Trivanti and Psion Infomedia have been added more recently. They have grown up from the bottom, coming out of what we call the nursery. All our businesses concentrate on mobile information and very much focus on specific links in the mobile Internet value-chain so:

- Psion Computers, market-leader in consumer and corporate palmtop computing, delivers solutions to mobile users with a growing range of wireless information devices
- Psion Connect, in PC card technologies, delivers access to Internet and corporate networks from any location
- Psion Teklogix works in partnership to provide powerful enterprise solutions for commerce and industry
- Psion Trivanti develops partnerships to deliver end-to-end solutions for mobile Internet users
- Psion Infomedia focuses on interactive entertainment and information appliances
- Symbian Limited, formerly Psion Software, is developing and marketing Epoc as the industry-standard operating software for the next generation of mobile communication and computing devices

We build on platforms leveraging our skills and brand values in our continual drive for breakthrough. This division of Psion's businesses has proved to be an ideal combination of brand image and competency skill set. There is a virtuous circle associated with the brand. Psion (if summed up as product development, R&D activity, philosophy and communications) constantly reinforces the 'dynamic IT company' perception that people have of us, thereby enabling us to hire the right people to constantly deliver these products, values and know-how to our customers.

Sharing our crown jewels

Every five years or so we reinvent ourselves. Now we are focusing on the fusion of the mobile phone and the hand-held computer. With communications increasingly central for our business and personal lives, it was essential our offer should evolve and that communications should be at the heart of the brand. The hand-held computer will converge with the cellphone into something we are calling the wireless information device. There are about 400 million cellphone subscribers worldwide, a figure that is projected to reach a billion – or one in six people on the planet – by 2002. Over the next five years these billion people will become increasingly data-enabled – shopping, accessing share prices and work on the Internet. It is all about portability, ubiquity and accessing services and transactions. It is an immense marketing opportunity.

Today Psion has roughly a third of the world's hand-held computer market, and nearly 40 per cent of the total UK market. However the real strength of Psion – our crown jewels – is what's inside: Epoc. The Psion iconic operating system with its modest power and memory requirements proved so successful that in 1998 we established a separate company, Symbian to adapt Epoc for use in other hand-held platforms, specifically in the wireless communications field.

The common purpose of all these devices is principally to provide Internet access on demand in any location, instead of being confined to PC. It is the wireless Internet, making information available wherever you are. We believe the Internet, not the PC, holds the key to the next stage of the information revolution and that, now as the PC and mobile worlds are merging, the mobile world will dominate. Hand-helds as Psion has known them will disappear, which is why we are forming such a central part of the mobile world now. We created Symbian to bring the wireless players together with our software experience to make palm-top, highly portable computer products. We bring our powerful brand values and know-how to work with those of our partners.

It is about establishing the winning operating system, which is why we are working in partnership with so many different organizations – content providers, media, hardware manufacturers and wireless services suppliers – to ensure that the end result is the most effective for the user. We were determined not to build a device that would be used solely by computer nerds – which was a risk if we had worked in isolation.

Our Epoc software is a terrifically well-written, multi-tasking, real-time solution and has no loss of time in starting up. It needed to be extraordinary to have the players we are working with all signing up to it. It could prove highly lucrative. If Epoc is the standard selected operating platform for the new handsets, Symbian will make $5–10 revenue on each of the 350 million smart-phones or communicators that it is anticipated will be sold. 80 per cent of the world's handset suppliers have signed up to it and Psion owns 28 per cent of Symbian.

We, of course, do not have the field to ourselves. Our main competitor is Microsoft with its Windows CE operating system, but as Windows CE is a cut-down version of their big PC software it is, in my view, inherently unstable. It is a question of where you come from: at Psion we built our devices with low power, low memory and limited operating power – they have to be very efficient and able to work in a rugged, robust and mobile environment. We are obviously onto something (hence Bill Gates' famous leaked memo, which identified Psion/Symbian as one of the greatest threats to his corporate empire).

It is a challenging and exciting time. Being so closely connected with the major global names in the industry, via Symbian, can cause ripples at Psion. On the whole it is of great benefit for us to leverage the strengths of the combined force. Our fortunes are however interconnected. If one of the partners has a handset shortage, Psion suffers too; if they hedge their bets by talking to one of our major competitors our share price halves immediately – it really is symbiosis! On the other hand, we enable the market by all playing in it. It will be thirty-five times as big as the entire sales of the handheld market since 1984.

Developing a powerful brand presence

Our policy has been for everything to be branded Psion. Our logo was launched before the organizer to communicate that we are a software company and the transformation of the letters into another form reflects transforming data into information.

We created the word organizer because we had to market and sell something that was completely new; we needed a name which was descriptive and emotive. We were trying to sell the function knowing it was a generic term and that we could not retain it for ever but the short-term benefit of it was a good one. Psion owned the category.

Once Psion had become generic for the organizer, we had a challenge when we moved into other areas such as PC cards. By becoming ubiquitous the Psion name did, however, open doors and we evolved effectively into 'the world leader in palmtop computing'. The reliability, adaptability and accessibility have won through consistently, whatever the product area or customer group.

All products have been branded Psion with the descriptive words downplayed hence Organizer Series 3 etc. as with BMW, the focus has always been to build the brand not the products. The brand identity features consistently on every product. Each product line is differentiated by a descriptor, so the Psion Organizer was followed by the Organizer II, the Series 3, the 3a, the Series 5, the Series 7, and several alphabetic and numeric permutations in-between.

We have concentrated at Psion on what we do well – the science, the design, the specification and the marketing. Significantly, the 'box-building' itself we have now out-sourced under licence.

The role of the corporate brand is a source of much discussion, particularly between the headquarters and the divisions, where the importance of keeping the values of the Psion brand consistent is constantly underlined. We think we have a brand that is worth more than the size of the company. But, although it is an asset, we don't lean on it too heavily. What we try to do is produce something that can compete in other respects, particularly performance. We are not a commodity or low-cost supplier, and we will always compete on differentiation, through market innovation, always doing something that's new and ahead of its time.

We are flexible on the development and communication of each range. Each company and many of the products which they market target quite different audiences, giving us an eternal challenge – being end-customer focused while protecting overall brand equities. Our solution is to consider every opportunity on its own merits. One complicating factor is that a global approach is essential, with 70 per cent of our sales outside the UK. Psion was initially a European phenomenon, and it was big in the Far East before the US.

We are constantly grappling with the challenges of growth. For example, Psion has only been divisionalized since 1996, as we came to see the wisdom of having semi-autonomous divisions. In addition, we have shifted from a system of country autonomy to one where products are managed across borders. There has been a battle with the country barons, which I think has been won by having the product companies in charge of the strategy.

It is interesting that only 6–7 per cent of our sales are in the US. The leaders in the wire-free market are Japan, followed by Europe and Asia. The US lags behind on wireless technology for a number of reasons:

– the wired network works well so there is far higher PC penetration in the US (unlike Japan, where the wired system is hopeless so take-up of wireless was faster)

- a competitive market has grown up in the US – not one with a standard, like Europe and Japan – so reception is not guaranteed (in which case it's hardly worth carrying a mobile around)
- there's a different payment structure – the receiver pays, so again you tend to keep it switched off and use a pager
- network coverage is an issue

We are a global company in the making and have to become one because of the nature of this industry. You need to be a certain scale if involved in technology. As a South African who has lived in the UK and US, I dislike jingoism. Psion needs to participate around the world. I hope it delivers that.

Fifteen years ago our marketing activities were quite disparate. As time has gone by, however, we have been able to coordinate activities more globally and therefore focus on the global brand. The logistics and control of distribution has been hugely enhanced. We now can control the entire brand across Europe as a whole and to an extent in the US too.

Growing the brand is an increasingly complex value chain

Business is becoming ever more complex. The two-dimensional value-chain, delivering a shirt to a customer, for example, was incredibly simple. The value-chain of a smart-phone is far more complicated. The technology providers, network operators, content and media providers are all inter-linked. In order to deliver the utility and functionality, companies have to work together much more intimately – mutual reliance and venturing are key elements of the new economy.

When it comes to branding and to whom you are aiming your branding, you have to analyse who your customers are and the best approach to reach them. Microsoft three years ago would have had 300 customer companies in the world; Symbian today only has

about twenty as only those twenty companies have the capability
of delivering the required technology.

It clearly made sense to give up the Psion name for Symbian.
Along with signalling a new era and being the only appropriate
action for branding a joint venture, it made the offer credible.
It ensured that the operating system could be spun off from the
hardware-creating part of Psion, thereby giving the operating
system credibility and enabling it to become the standard. We saw
and learned from the appalling strategic error Apple Computers
made by not splitting itself into two different outfits – the software
and the hardware – in the 1980s. If they had done so, they would
have been where Microsoft is without any doubt. Everyone would
have bought into it. Instead no one did – they saw it as a side issue
and Apple as a competitor.

The multi-dimensional value-chain is having an impact on distribution. In our traditional retailers the product is sold at a margin
and at price parity with other similar retailers. With the network
operators, the product is bundled within a more complex offer.
They sell the Psion device, a phone and a twelve-month contract.
Due to the value of the contract retailers subsidize the phone and
the Psion device. The consumer sees two very different propositions
in two stores, which can lead to significant channel management
problems.

There are positives however: the market has been hugely
expanded and Psion has been repositioned as complementary to
mobile phones by being sold bundled with them. It is a useful
stepping stone in terms of consumer perception as the next generation of Psion will include a phone component. The evolving
product also has implications for traditional retailers like Dixons
which are not yet structured to carry the next Psion devices.

A deep relationship is now essential with the network operators
– Orange, Vodafone and Deutsche Telecomm. Network operators
control access, and so they are the most powerful sellers of the
device itself. In most markets, people will see it as part of the offering. Network operators are limited to only a few top-tier operators
at present – the largest of whom is Nokia, with one third of the

market, followed by Ericsson and Motorola. They are keen to groom the next generation of hand-helds and this is a very interesting opportunity for us over the next couple of years. We have a kind of open door support from these giant organizations so will use our brand but with their channel and their strength.

Overall, it is a fascinating coopetition situation. We'll share one element but compete on another. With Epoc, the Symbian operating system, we all have a standard to work with but we all compete on the final products that will use that standard. The Symbian board is a fascinating one of which to be a part.

Developing and promoting the growth vision

The emphasis on generating new ideas comes from the top. I call it 'catching the next wave'. So there is an expectation among the group of senior managers that you have to find something new – this is part of our history.

Psion plans its strategy five years forward, which includes discussions about targets. But they are used more for illustration than as an expectation of hard and fast reality. We look at the divisions that we have now, and consider how they might grow, and we consider creating new divisions, for instance, but all of this is highly speculative. In a sense it is unlikely in five years' time to be exactly the way we planned, but our strategy lays down an intent of growth. It sets an environment of expectation that we are growing, and the shape of the group that we envisage. Being flexible is essential in technology, where developments such as the Internet can change the landscape dramatically and in a short space of time. I personally put a lot of effort into keeping ahead.

In terms of pursuing growth, we work on the principle that any market we are in today will get tougher for all kinds of reasons: it is very much a burning platform feeling. It gets tougher because if you have any success your competitors are on your back straight away.

For Psion, opportunities lie not so much in developing better technologies as in finding new market opportunities with technology. The environment is changing and will change in the future, so we look for a combination of the direction of the market and technology. For example, the Internet introduced new needs but we had to understand the trends in the technology and the marketplace before we could adapt to meet these needs. Development takes a year or so, and, in terms of the competencies, even longer; what is important is to do something in the light of a mega-trend before it is obvious to everybody else.

The biggest obstacle to growth is having enough of the right management, which tends to be a problem throughout the high-tech sector. It is a case of balancing the cost line against getting enough of the right people on board even before they are needed. Ideally you would hire an excess of the right people, but the right people are going to be expensive people. Having them sitting around 'twiddling their thumbs' until an opportunity comes along would obviously throw that balance out of line.

Sharing knowledge is part of Psion's culture, helped by the fact that the heads of the three big divisions are on the main board. However, we are aware that we have reached the stage where we have to address a number of issues that size implies. For example, we need to get even faster at making decisions and management development is another area which needs a more formal approach.

Coming up with innovative ideas is one of the company's critical capabilities. But improvements could be made in the more mechanistic side of things, or actually getting the products to market, although the company is addressing this as it grows.

Innovation – the core value and central challenge

What has worked for Psion has been the marrying of vision with commercial expertise. As we are an engineering-orientated company, it is very easy to fall into the trap of producing products that are too technologically driven and do not meet real needs. Here it is not so much marketing and engineering as commercial business people plus engineering. Whenever I have seen a success, there has been a pairing – and not always in the same person – of a technological visionary, who really understands the industry, with someone who has a commercial and entrepreneurial sense.

The key question as the organization gets bigger is whether or not it is possible to enshrine innovation, learning and change within a larger organization. Large organizations tend to be risk averse. Innovation is very difficult for them. There's a tendency in management to eliminate the essential conditions innovation thrives on. They are uncomfortable with mavericks and fail to recognize that if you try to eliminate all risk you also eliminate all opportunity. In general, human beings are uncomfortable with that which is new but the continuation of the genes of innovation is vital and it has to be built in as a core value driver. Grass roots and many small companies have got it. How do you keep it as you grow?

This is the biggest single strategic challenge for management. At Psion we created our divisions to ensure that we keep the spirit of innovation alive. The way we work enables us to do so too. Marketing textbooks and Proctor & Gamble can listen to consumers and respond accordingly. We have to adopt a different approach – with new technology it is beyond the realms of experience or aspiration. If we'd listened to our customers we wouldn't have half the products we have today.

We're a raft of people. We work in teams. We spend time analysing the process, and part of the challenge for us is to make it a systemized process. Large companies need to organize with systems and policies and processes. You can and need to structure things to an extent at a company like ours. You need understanding of future technology – technology foresight. We've got a team studying technology all the time: semi-conductor technology, voice recognition technology, spacial technology, wireless technology. These people interpret what it will all mean for us in three, five or ten years – how these technologies will become vastly more effective and cheaper and so on.

This is one driver. The other is to understand market needs, but not so much in the facile way of saying 'listen to your customers'.

We need to go beyond that in order to understand the behaviour and needs of customers at a different level. You couldn't ask them in 1988 if they might need a hand-held cellular phone when all they could see then was a large box with large batteries. You had to ask: 'what if you were able to communicate wherever you are? Would you like that?' Then you find that the requirements you need to build in are portability and longer battery life. We are looking at customer needs at a deeper level, and at human psychology.

With the organizer area, people didn't realize how much personal information they have or need and how important it was to them. Companies certainly do now. Many individuals have realized how key information is for them too. The make-up of individuals is quite varied however; the market breaks down into different kinds of people with different needs.

We could see that the utility and benefit that our devices would provide would apply to both the individual and corporate sphere. The question when you've something that's radical and very new is how do you establish channels and awareness of the utility and function. That's why we created the word 'organizer'.

To us in 1983, the year before we launched the product, and while our work was going on, it was clear there were potentially two markets. We could launch it in a number of different ways. By going pretty rugged for a whole variety of markets and launching to the individual too we hit both markets. By having a very wide campaign at a fairly superficial level we announced it very widely and this indeed produced the leads to the corporate sector as well. It captured the imagination. We were conscious of both opportunities and wished to exploit both.

We also examine competitors and all the usual things. On that score I believe 'pull' is best. Looking over your shoulder at competitors is pointless. By the time you get there it'll be so passé you'll have had it. It is fine as a marketing process for a different kind of company but not in our sector. Other companies need to be behind the wave. We certainly cannot be.

We benchmark too, companies such as Hewlett-Packard or Sony

or Motorola. All three have been able to innovate again and again and again. They may all go through good and bad periods but they have (and continue) to build themselves upon innovation over a long period of time.

I hope Psion can continue to be an innovative company and that we can nurture that value system. From that point of view, splitting off Psion Software to become Symbian was challenging – we needed to keep and develop breakthrough capabilities in-house too. It proved to be an incredibly energy-sapping time; we were designing the Series 5 organizer at the time. Psion Software moved out to become Symbian and the hardware formed the Series 5.

We therefore had two start-ups in February 1999 to reignite the company. There'd been stagnation and blockage – products in development for a long time. Share of mind of management needed to come out of the lab and into the field. The start-ups were learning platforms. It's our biggest challenge. We must never lose that heart of our being.

Our future

While not denying the strength of the competition, I am convinced that Psion will continue to play a defining role. The market broadly agrees although, from time to time, the company has fallen out of favour with investors, fearful that the sheer brute force and scale of our American rivals will snuff us out.

There have been difficult times when the company has been under pressure, but that's part of business. My colleagues see me as being very conservative financially – we follow a prudent financial policy in contrast to the adventurous markets we are engaged in. One of the reasons we have survived is that we don't have any borrowings.

It feels like we are in the right place at the right time. We may be a small fish but it's a huge pond and we intend to contribute to it and capitalize upon it.

Commentary

The Psion story highlights the importance of combining engineering and creative excellence with sound commercial nous. There is a practicality and pragmatism which, combined with the focus of enquiring minds, ensures Psion delivers and continues to deliver products that are useful, practical and wanted.

There is a way of working that seems to work well for its market – consumer research but in the correct context: it is so far beyond possibility and aspiration that it needs to be set in the right context. The same is true for Psion of benchmarking. It is not about what the great innovators are up to but how they have done it time and time again.

The global branding approach has also worked effectively. Linking the name with the generic organizer served only to make Psion a household name, not to reduce its potency as it moved into new sectors or markets. And catering for both consumer and commercial markets has also worked powerfully in the brand's growth. There is a strong cohesion across the two markets, a blurring of barriers, so increasingly what works at home can be tailored for in the workplace and vice versa. Increasingly they are one and the same and Psion is well-placed to facilitate how people work and play.

The Psion approach to partnership and coopetition is also one which works to differentiate the company from the crowd. By splitting out Psion Software as the joint venture, Symbian credibility is given to Psion's crown jewels and the expertise comes on board to help establish Epoc as the winning platform.

Psion looks set to go from strength to strength provided as David Potter stresses their approach to innovation can remain intact and grow in line with company and market needs.

5 | Reuters: Transforming the Brand for the Information Age

PETER JOB, *chief executive, and*
JEAN-CLAUDE MARCHAND, *chairman and group marketing director*

Reuters has transformed itself from a global news agency to a global business information provider and is embarking on the next stage of transformation as it exploits the Internet as a new delivery vehicle for its products. Peter Job, chief executive, and Jean-Claude Marchand, chairman and group marketing director, explain how.

As the world's leading news and financial information organization, Reuters starts with some formidable brand assets. According to the Interbrand branding agency, it is the most valuable brand in the UK. Its reputation for independence, integrity and impartiality goes back for 150 years. The idea of the Reuters correspondent going to the ends of the earth and bringing the news back first strikes a chord with populations across the world. Even in rural China, the name of Reuters is known – there is a Chinese expression for it (meaning 'whispers on the street corner').

In its main activity – as a vendor of financial information supported by advanced technology – it is a clear market leader in most parts of the world. It is unrivalled in the scope, sophistication and depth of information that it supplies to banks, to the media and increasingly also to other businesses and private individuals. With some 2,150 journalists, photographers and camera people operating from 190 bureaux, it deploys one of the strongest forces in the world for gathering and disseminating news.

We are now living in an information-driven society, and Reuters is positioned as one of the most respected sources. It provides information and technology to help people make decisions crucial for their business and private lives. Above all people believe us.

All of the world's leading banks, brokers and other financial institutions use Reuters information to trade on markets. Top companies use it to research markets and competitors, and the media throughout the world use it to create newspapers and television and radio programmes. Individuals can now use Reuters information to manage their personal finances on the Internet.

So Reuters has many of the components of a major global brand in one of the most exciting and promising industries of today and tomorrow. When Interbrand made its latest calculations in July 2000, it valued the Reuters brand at $4.9 billion, representing about 15 per cent of our market capitalization at the time. It placed us second globally among media businesses, and overall the forty-sixth in the world.

However, as it celebrates its 150th anniversary in 2001, Reuters too faces a number of branding challenges as the Internet and other new information technologies change the shape of the world.

Reuters' branding challenge

To start with, what exactly *is* Reuters? Few people would be able to give anything like the wide-ranging description of our activities explained above. Despite the fact that the company has been building its financial markets business at often very fast rates of growth over the last twenty-eight years, most people know Reuters just as a news agency. They know that we provide news and photos to newspapers, and assume that this is our sole business. At a time when Reuters is poised to penetrate a much expanded online market for financial market professionals and private investors through the Internet, our market research is showing that only a small percentage of the general public know that we have anything to do with finance. That is quite a branding challenge.

So where do we come from? The other fact which a fair number of people know about Reuters – and are intrigued and fascinated by – is that our founder, Paul Julius Reuter, began business flying information from one place to another by pigeon. In 1849 there was a gap in the telegraph line between Aachen and Brussels. So stock prices being transmitted between the Berlin and Paris stock exchanges had to be sent over this stretch by a very slow train. Reuter used pigeons to fly the prices faster and secure a competitive advantage. It was a brilliant example of improvisation and innovation, which, however, lasted for just a couple of years until the missing telegraph line was installed. And that's when Reuters history really started.

To appreciate Reuters and its brand, you have to understand its history. Paul Julius Reuter moved to London and established his news agency there in 1851. He quickly gained a reputation as a prime source of fast, accurate and unbiased foreign news, and for imaginative use of information technology. At the time, that meant the telegraph, and the Reuters motto, implemented with growing success, was 'follow the cable'. In today's world of the Internet and wireless application protocols (WAP), this inspiring idea is still very largely relevant. What goes around comes around.

But until the 1960s, Reuters *was* essentially a news agency. In the 1970s, it transformed itself through bold pioneering ventures which created a range of electronic information products for the world's rapidly growing financial markets. It first revolutionized foreign exchange trading by giving dealers access to real-time rates and news on Reuters Monitor computer terminals. It followed in 1981 with the launch of electronic transactions over the Reuters network, which again changed practices in this market. This led to rapid growth in the company's revenues and profits, and a high level of development investment enabled Reuters to pioneer electronic broking systems, multimedia in financial trading rooms, massive financial databases, and most recently, applications of Internet technologies.

Reuters became a public listed company and was floated on the London Stock Exchange and Nasdaq in New York in 1984. By late 2000, it was the seventeenth most valuable company on the London Stock Exchange by market capitalization.

Reuters has offices in 204 cities in 100 countries, with staff or just over 18,000. It has currently some 558,000 users at 50,600 locations in 151 countries. Today, over 93 per cent of Reuters revenue comes from the financial markets, all over the world. Besides the public Internet, Reuters uses one of the world's largest private communications networks, now being progressively converted to Internet protocols in collaboration with our Equant communications partner.

So this is a distinguished record of innovation and bold entrepreneurship in the world's financial markets, built on a solid foundation of trust and longevity. But public awareness of the special qualities of the Reuters brand does not run very deep.

Reuters statutes prevent any shareholder from owning 15 per cent or more shares in the company, and Reuters Trust Principles provide further safeguards of independence and integrity. The Principles are backed by a Founder's Share which can out-vote all other ordinary shares.

For much of its history, Reuters has felt no great need to promote its brand. We were confident in our reputation for independence, integrity, impartiality and reliability, which were well established as core values held in high esteem by our customers.

There was a wholesale nature to the business model. Often, the person with whom we would do business was a bank's IT manager, and the counterpart on the Reuters side was a sales person. Functionality, product upgrades, competitive advantage for the customer institution and cost were the main issues driving the business relationship.

However, IT managers after a time did not just want to plug in Reuters terminals linked to our network. They wanted to integrate Reuters information and added-value software into the ever more complex high-performance systems they were building inside the banks. Reuters met this demand by providing datafeeds instead of terminals and embracing the philosophy of 'open systems'. It was the right decision, since it addressed the customers' wants and needs, and gave us an even stronger competitive position vis-à-vis rivals who were slower to move this way. But the price of this was a loss of branding. The distinctive rows of branded Reuters screens in dealing rooms gave way to a diverse array of systems where the Reuters name faded into the background.

Success also bred stronger competition. In Reuters' mainstream financial markets business, the number of competitors is not large, but there are one or two companies which do not hesitate to use aggressive brand promotion to push their way into our markets.

In our traditional news agency market of newspapers and broadcasting, brand exposure derived from credits could no longer be counted on as much as in the past. In the old days, a Reuters dispatch was often the only source of foreign news. Improving communications systems make it easier for others to provide such news. Computerized editing systems in newspapers enable sub-editors to merge Reuters news easily into reports from their own journalists or other sources. Often the Reuters credit is sacrificed in favour of the newspaper's own branding – 'from our own correspondent'.

In supermarket terms, it is like the perpetual conflict between the established brand (Reuters) and own-label offerings.

Television has also become a more important source of news for many people, and there branding is *all* 'own-label'. Reuters has always been the wholesaler, and most television stations reject any attempt to admit our branding. Few people know that a large part of the foreign news film they see on their evening television programmes comes from Reuters. Our name does not appear.

The Internet changes all that

The Internet represented a significant potential threat to our business. Financial information which previously was only available on the Reuters network is now much more freely available. But the Internet also opens vast new opportunities for Reuters, not least in branding. In recent years, we have been rapidly building up our news presence on websites all over the Internet. With a presence on over 1,400 sites reaching an estimated 73 million viewers per month, Reuters is the principal supplier of news to the World Wide Web.

In this Internet environment, partners are much readier to publish Reuters credits. The news helps keep a website active and attractive, so that viewers keep coming back. But it only does that if the source has prestige and is trusted. The Internet is also a great pool of rumour and fraudulently misleading information. The Reuters credentials count for a guarantee of quality and reliability in an environment where such attributes cannot automatically be counted on.

Digital television stations operating on the Internet or telecommunications channels often welcome the opportunity to brand the digital multimedia output of an established player such as Reuters. They have much lower cost structures than traditional television stations, and their business models do not need a powerful 'own-label' brand.

This is not just an Internet phenomenon. Partly it is a factor of geography and political history. In Russia and eastern Europe, for example, our brand is much more readily acknowledged and valued. During the Cold War, populations knew the name of Reuters as one of the few sources of trusted news about their own countries. Western radios broadcasting to these countries often quoted Reuters correspondents living in their midst. When political regimes and markets opened up in the early 1990s, Reuters was immediately a trusted partner in a new world which was often harsh and chaotic.

But the new world of the Internet and mobile communications is also forcing companies like Reuters to become more marketing-driven and use the brand as a fundamental weapon in its business armoury. The field may be more open to us for branding, but it also allows a host of competitors to do the same. On the Internet, a brand profile does not fall into your lap. You have to fight for it.

Now Reuters is on the Net too, and the same goes for us. We are moving to take a more aggressive stance in our branding.

A new business model

In February 2000, Reuters announced a series of bold new initiatives to exploit the Internet and open new markets, reinforced by a number of joint ventures in communications, wireless delivery and investment research.

These initiatives convinced people that Reuters had an imaginative and credible strategy for the Internet. Inside Reuters, the changes have also been deeply felt, since our business model is changing radically. There was an immediate buzz of enthusiasm, a sense of excitement, that Reuters is heading full-tilt into a world where it has every chance to succeed.

For the Internet is a natural environment for Reuters. We have been building electronic communities around real-time information for thirty years. Our vision now is to 'make financial markets really work on the Internet'.

'Really'? Yes, because a sea of raw information surging around the Internet is not enough to make financial markets really function in their environment. You need the skill to gather the right information, and select and display it in ever more sophisticated ways for different groups of users. You need to be able to analyse the information, and then rapidly and easily access pools of liquidity in the markets where the best prices can be found. Above all, you need a reputation of trust based on truthfulness. That's exactly where Reuters core competencies lie.

Reuters is now moving rapidly to an e-business model – in product development, delivery, administration and support. The Internet is opening the way for us to create online communities of professional market participants and private investors. Before, the costs of development, selling, support and delivery were relatively high, so cost limited the potential market for Reuters services. Now, the Internet brings all these costs down, and Reuters can tap large new markets with lower-priced offerings. We estimate over 65 million people will be using the Internet for financial business of one kind or another in the near future.

It is about linking the process of 'knowing' to 'doing', in a few seconds or, at most, a few minutes. And all of this now available not just in financial trading rooms, but potentially also directly in people's living rooms.

Banks themselves move information around their newly-created intranets. Again, an opportunity for Reuters, which before could not cost-effectively reach customer-facing staff and back offices who had only an occasional need for market information. Now Reuters serves these people with smaller, specially-tailored packages of information piped at minimal cost through their company intranets. This represents not only a new source of revenue, but also a new opportunity to spread the name of Reuters more widely and obtain world-of-mouth recommendation.

The banks often want to make Reuters information available directly to their own clients on the Internet. Reuters provides the information and the Web facilities to do this. Reuters' Web-farm serves this rapidly growing clientele, and with over 400 million hits per month has become one of Europe's busiest financial Internet sites.

Brand: the plan of action

The new business strategy focusing on the Internet has had a revitalising effect on the Reuters brand, increasing its position as a major global force. Reliance on highly skilled sales people as the main interface with the outside world is no longer sufficient. With the new business model, face-to-face contact cannot be the only means of penetrating potential markets numbering tens of millions rather than a few hundred thousand.

Our sales team remains an important asset, however, since customers often benefit from counselling to find the right mix of Reuters products to match their exact requirements. But Reuters is now also using more of the marketing techniques of consumer and Internet businesses – advertising, public relations, direct marketing, community building, channel marketing, affiliations and partnerships.

We began our brand development programme in 1996, when we did our first in-depth review of the Reuters brand ahead of a re-modelling of the Reuters visual identity – the corporate logo – working with brand consultants Landor and subsequently with Lambie-Nairn. This resulted in the formal expression of our core values and a new visual identity.

Since 1965 the Reuters logo had spelt out the Reuters name in dots. At the time it was original and distinctive, but by the 1990s it was too redolent of old-fashioned telex ticker-tape. Worse still, it failed to stand out, in particularly on video-screens. Since the first task of a visual identity is to be visible, we joined up the dots so that the Reuters name stood out clearly and emphatically. The dots reappeared in a sphere symbolising day-and-night operations, global ubiquity and openness.

The next step in brand development was brand advertising, which began in 1998 in the five countries that are our most important markets – the US, the UK, Germany, Japan and Switzerland. The end-line of the first campaign 'Reuters. The Truth. Deal with it' underlined the company's reputation for accuracy and trustworthiness and its usefulness in financial trading. Although our initial media spends were relatively modest, research showed that our advertising had had the desired effect of bringing this vital attribute to the forefront of people's minds.

As the company swung more decisively to the Internet, however, we moved to a new message which made the Reuters brand relevant to the new generation of professionals and private investors working in this environment. Many of these people had little or no experience of Reuters more sophisticated financial products, which had been confined largely to trading rooms because of network costs. Yet, Reuters was already highly visible on the Internet, and it was time to talk about it, loudly.

Before moving ahead, we re-examined our brand positioning in interviews with senior managers and customers worldwide. Reuters' reputation for truthfulness was clearly well established, but customer feedback showed that this was not enough as a sole differentiator in their choice of brand. There was also a pressing need for Reuters to profile itself more forcefully in the dot-com world. Too few people were aware of our dynamic and imaginative initiatives in this area.

So we developed a new brand proposition which emphasized the particularly competitive attributes of Reuters and added a sense of speed and excitement. The proposition encapsulated in the phrase 'Reuters. Where the action is' puts our brand onto the front foot and lets us go on to the offensive. It highlights the aspects where Reuters is truly ahead of our rivals, such as our leading role in the world's financial trading rooms, and the global scope of our coverage and support infrastructure on the ground.

In journalistic terms, it means our reporters and camera people who operate in zones such as Kosovo or Sierra Leone. Or our financial journalists, who cover interest rate changes where absolute accuracy is imperative, and a few seconds' advantage or delay can spell millions of dollars of profit or loss for our customers.

Reuters is also 'where the action is' in providing information and key components to more than half the world's top online brokerage sites. As the top provider of news on the World Wide Web, Reuters is moving in the vanguard of share trading reform through our electronic trading subsidiary Instinet, and is developing Internet software through our TIBCO associate company in Palo Alto. Our slogan therefore reflects what Reuters has been doing for 150 years – placing skilled experts where world events are unrolling and pioneering the use of the latest methods of communication.

We asked our advertising agency BMP/DDB to develop the creative idea behind the brand proposition, making it relevant to the online private investor audience we particularly want to reach. The texts ask a series of questions which widen perceptions of our activities, and to which the answer is always 'Reuters. Behind Every Decision'. The ads show how Reuters plays a key role in our customers' decision making – in ways they had not imagined before. The style is contemporary and upbeat. Beneath a striking image of criss-crossing railway lines, we ask: 'Who delivers information to all of the world's most popular online brokerages?' The answer: 'Reuters. Behind Every Decision'.

In 2000, we decided to do our first television advertising. We began with a commercial which by its size and scope was designed to emphasize Reuters' potential global brand stature. It is a parable along the lines of Noah, in which the hero anticipates a flood through information which enables him to save his pet-shop animals and make a financial profit. He obtains the information online from Reuters – 'Behind Every Decision'.

To reinforce this image of a new, more dynamic company, at ease in the dot-com world, we built up a network of public relations agencies in thirteen countries. Public relations is for Reuters an efficient and cost-effective means of putting across messages about the company which are of necessity sometimes complex, and pushing the Reuters name towards the 'top-of-mind' position which all brands aims for.

As a next step we decided to use another marketing tool, sponsorship. Although we had sponsored various activities on a small scale for some years, we now chose an initiative which would demonstrate Reuters' new dynamism and vitality with maximum impact (and ear-splitting noise). We also selected it because we knew it was popular with our existing customers and with the new ones we want to attract on the Net. Since the beginning of 2000, Reuters has been co-sponsoring the BMW Williams F1 Team in formula one Grand Prix motor racing. It is an excellent fit for a brand on the move: it is all about speed, adrenalin, leading-edge technology, and reliability. It is also a truly global sport with seventeen races in fifteen countries over nine months of every year. It is one of the most popular televised sports in the world, attracting audiences of over 300 million for each race.

Tobacco sponsors are becoming rarer in Formula One motor racing, and Reuters is among a number of financial and high-tech companies which are moving in to take their place. We find ourselves among other newcomers such as Crédit Suisse, HSBC, Compaq, Nortel networks, Intel, Orange and Hewlett-Packard. We feel ourselves in the right company. Apart from the external impact, this new sponsorship also had a galvanizing effect on our own staff, coming as it did just a few weeks before the announcement of our enterprising new business strategy.

To reinforce this initial high-impact entry into major sponsorship, we have targeted other sponsorships at the 65 million people we believe will be using the Internet to conduct financial business, professionally or for themselves. We want to reach these individuals through sponsoring the sort of sports they typically like to practise, such as golf, skiing and yachting.

Through the Reuters Foundation, our charitable arm, we further increase our profile by sponsoring a series of educational and humanitarian projects, mostly linked with information. An outstanding example is Alertnet, an Internet site run by the Foundation on which humanitarian relief agencies can exchange and find information when disasters strike, enabling them to target their efforts more effectively. The Reuters Foundation operates on a budget of around £3.3 million.

For Reuters, the brand is Reuters. We have noticed that many users refer to the product they use as just 'my Reuters'. So we have decided on a basically monolithic brand structure, that is, all the brand equity is loaded into the Reuters name and product names are for the most part purely descriptive. There are only a few exceptions, where a product name has built its own brand equity.

Purely descriptive names clarify what each product does and how it potentially fits together with another product. This is much welcomed by our customers, and helps our sales force too. The inter-connectivity of our products is becoming increasingly valuable to our customers – this extra clarity is an important business asset.

The future

In branding, the sky's the limit. One never reaches the summit. There is always more to be done. Brands need constant nurturing and the ability to adapt to changing market conditions. Behind the smart communication, there must be solid achievement in innovation to meet customers' changing needs and wants with products they want to buy. There is no room for complacency.

However, after 150 years of existence, Reuters is assuredly on the threshold of the most exciting period of its colourful history. The Internet and new wireless technologies open the way for the company to potentially hugely broaden its markets.

Reuters sets off on this exciting road with a wealth of trust attached to its brand – perhaps the single most important brand value for any business in the new economy of the twenty-first century. With a dynamic new business strategy which is radically transforming the company, Reuters is at the leading edge – ahead of the field, where our journalists and engineers first began carving our reputation one and a half centuries ago.

Commentary

Reuters has used technology to transform the core-product offering of the brand. It is drawn on the invaluable brand heritage of trust-worthiness, breadth of coverage and accuracy with the added-on contemporary values of speed, ease of use and modernity. As such it carries a much enhanced brand reputation in comparison with the new entrants who can offer similar product performance but lack Reuters' pedigree and reputation.

Reuters also exemplifies the importance of watching ahead for technological change rather than reacting to change when it happens. In this case, Reuters has been able to develop Internet-enabled products quickly and effectively and plan carefully for their delivery to existing customers and to new customers by opening up new market segments. The use of a marketing periscope to assess technological change and customer attitudes has never been so important.

6 | Sony: Re-inventing Itself to Keep Ahead in the Networked World

JEAN-MICHEL PERBET, *president and chief operating officer*

Sony has built strong market positions and a powerful brand reputation across Europe. However it recognized that the market was changing and therefore set about vigorous reappraisal of everything it did.

Jean-Michel Perbet, president and COO of Sony Europe, explains the reasoning behind the company's changes.

Current market position

Initially, when Sony was established in Tokyo in the mid-1940s, its products (for both business and private users) were sold only in Japan. The company soon moved to distribute them in Europe and North America, where their combination of innovation and technical excellence greatly contributed to their success. By the 1960s Sony had become an international standard bearer for Japanese industry.

Sony revolutionized the home electronics markets around the world with products such as the first truly pocket-sized transistor radio, the Walkman personal stereo and the Trinitron colour television. In the 1980s it developed the Compact Disc format with Philips of the Netherlands and began to expand into market sectors outside its traditional audio-visual base. A few years ago Sony launched a successful range of notebook computers under the VAIO (Video Audio Integrated Operation) model name; it has recently marketed a distinctive line of mobile phones, digital still cameras and video cameras; with the PlayStation and the recently launched PlayStation 2 it is the strongest force in the fast-growing video games console market. And it still services the needs of the world's broadcasters and institutional users with state-of the art digital technologies and products.

Furthermore, Sony has expanded its operations to encompass businesses in the areas of films and TV programme production and distribution, music and video games.

The changing marketplace

Sony recognizes that the audio and video markets and the information technology market are rapidly converging, driven by the evolution of digital technologies. This convergence represents an exciting and substantial opportunity for us.

Ever more powerful computer chips have become the norm in televisions and video cameras, while desk-top and notebook computers are being used to download and playback music and videos from the Internet, manipulate digital images and edit home videos. As PCs are being used more and more in the home, it is becoming increasingly easy to link technologies together. In only a few years, we at Sony believe that the distinction between the audio, video and information technology markets will become less and less clear: instead there will be one main market, which we call AV-IT.

Sony can claim to be one of the few companies, if not the only company, in the world which is involved in the creation of all aspects of entertainment, producing films, TV programmes, video games, music and of course the electronic products themselves. We believe we can enhance this competitive advantage over time. As the digital revolution will spread, Sony will be at the leading edge of change.

Three years ago Sony Corporation announced a new structure for the company worldwide and a three-year investment plan aimed at preparing the group for new challenges. As our then President Nobuyuki Idei said, 'The group will invest aggressively in R&D,

capital equipment and facilities so that our electronics business, which is our core business, can evolve to best meet the needs of a network-centric world. We are committed to creating new lifestyles and providing new forms of enjoyment to people in the network-centric society of the twenty-first century.'

Sony allows its constituent parts considerable autonomy. While corporate headquarters in Japan develops the overarching global strategy, it is up to the regional management to work out how best to execute and implement the strategy in each market. After all it was Sony who coined the phrase 'think global, act local'.

Sony in Europe

Our first European operations date back to the early 1960s with the establishment of Sony Overseas in Switzerland but this was largely a finance operation since the distribution of Sony products was handled through agents or dealers. We established a subsidiary in the UK in 1968, in Germany in 1970, and France in 1973. Other countries followed over the years and today Europe accounts for 22–24 per cent of worldwide sales. As our European operations grew in size, local manufacturing plants were established in Wales, France, Austria and Spain, to name a few countries.

In October last year, coinciding with the relocation of the European headquarters to Berlin, Sony Europe announced a new organization structure to direct our European business activities in the new millennium. An important part of our new structure was the creation of business units with full responsibility for pricing, profit and loss and manufacturing activities on a European consolidated basis – to name but a few of their responsibilities.

The result of these changes was that local marketing staff now report to the Europe-wide business groups. In addition, there is a newly established European sales structure to supplement local sales personnel and to address the needs of cross-border buying groups. Retailers are expanding across Europe, and our sales organization could no longer be based on national market focus. We are also harmonizing our terms and conditions of sale across Europe as far as is practicable (given continuing differences in local law and practice). This whole process will enable us to standardize our product lines across Europe, with of course some flexibility for local variations, thus reflecting consumer needs.

Although there will continue to be cosmetic differences in the exact product specifications required by consumers in different European countries, these are no longer as significant as they once were. Consumer needs and demands are becoming much more homogenous across Europe, as cross-border media and travel increase, as digital technology spreads, as local trading conditions align to a single market and as pan-European retailing chains emerge. In particular, the core Sony target market of young, affluent, educated, sophisticated and technology-friendly individuals have a lot in common across national boundaries. In short, we could look at a market divided amongst related product sectors without the added complexity of geographic divisions dictating our product offering.

Developing the new marketing strategy

As the AV-IT opportunity and challenge emerged, Sony Europe embarked on a simultaneous strategy review to assess its position in the enlarged market. The objective was, to develop a strategy to persuade existing and potential purchasers of the new possibilities being created by digital technology in general, and by the Sony range in particular.

An in-depth independent brand audit research programme carried out across Europe during 1999 showed that Sony was viewed by the majority of European consumers as the King of AV and brand awareness in our existing product categories was excellent. This study clearly showed that we have many advantages. We have a heritage of successful innovation, notably in camcorders, personal hi-fis and televisions and we have a reputation for stylish product design.

Nearly two-thirds of all European consumers polled said they were either quite interested or very interested in using digital technology but in almost every market the majority admitted knowing very little about either the technology or its products. Further research showed that the potentially revolutionary benefits which digital technology offers were only understood by a very small minority of Europeans. For most digital simply means better – better sound or better pictures and not yet a revolution in connectivity.

In summary, the research showed that consumers viewed Sony as a successful innovator, with a strong brand heritage in AV products. Consumers were also showing considerable interest in digital technology but, as yet, little understanding of what it really offered. Most importantly the research confirmed that convergence would bring Sony face to face with a new set of competitors from the IT industry.

What we needed to do was revolutionize the way that consumers think about the new world of entertainment in the AV-IT era and how Sony fits into it. We explored a number of different positionings of which the clear winner in research was 'creativity/ open minds'. There was strong consumer evidence that a brand positioning based on communicating and reinforcing the different ways in which Sony's technical superiority can provide new experiences would have real influence and consumer appeal.

We needed to clearly differentiate the brand from existing AV competition while also giving an opportunity to make a pre-emptive claim for leadership of the emerging AV-IT market – ahead of potential new competitors from the IT world. The core strategic message, which was developed, is a simple one: 'Sony – the inspiration to do more'.

As I have already observed, convergence is here, driven by new digital technologies, and the AV and IT markets are undergoing fundamental changes. But, while consumers are vaguely aware of digital technology and know that it is having an effect on things such as mobile phones, television, radio and photography, most cannot define what 'digital' actually means, and most do not know which products are digital and which are not. And while consumers may well want to use AV-IT products, they do not as yet have any language to describe what they want to do and how they want to do it.

Despite this lack of language, consumers certainly need AV-IT products. We have in Europe an increasingly time-poor, cash-rich, mobile population which desperately wants to make human connections. They are hungry for richer experiences and want to do more with their leisure time. They want to communicate.

At present, however, it is only the early adopters or innovators – a small group of consumers – who are using AV-IT to anything like its full potential. This will soon change. Over the next few years AV-IT will become a mainstream marketplace as audio and video consumers migrate to digital equipment and discover the possibilities they offer. Sony must be the first brand to make the desire to buy digital equipment – to use AV-IT as a creative tool – mainstream. For example, it must become as natural to consumers to use their Sony VAIO to edit a video, which they shot on their Sony camcorder and to send it to their friends and family on the Internet as it is to take a snapshot and sending a print by post today.

The VAIO, with its leading-edge capabilities, its slim, light and stylish design and its convergence-ready technology, offers users productivity without limitation of place – the ability to create possibilities wherever they are. The Sony MiniDisc, which features re-recordable discs, the ability to edit music and digital quality sound in a rugged and portable package, offers consumers their own mix of music when and where they want it. The compact, stylish Sony Cyber-Shot Digital Stills camera takes high-quality digital photos (and digital video images which you can easily transfer to a PC via a 'memory stick' recordable storage device or an iLINK single cable connection), so you can share your pictures with friends or colleagues.

An advertising campaign on its own is, of course, useless without the mould-breaking products to back it up. Sony has those products. For the past few years our research and development people have been working on a whole range of products that offer easy connectivity through the medium of the revolutionary 'memory stick'. This recordable storage device, about the size of a pack of chewing gum, can be used in cameras, computers, voice recorders and other products. It can carry up to 64 megabytes of data – the equivalent of around 60 floppy discs. All the consumer needs to do is to take the memory stick out of one appliance and slot it into another, and the data it contains can be used as desired. There are currently over thirty products which can use the memory stick, not all of which are made by Sony, as there are currently 120 memory stick licensees worldwide.

The 'Go Create' campaign

In the autumn of 1999 we appointed Saatchi & Saatchi as the lead agency to handle our consumer electronics products advertising in Europe. The brief was to develop an advertising strategy which we could use across all the European markets in which we are active. The resulting 'Go Create' campaign has now been running in twenty-five countries across Europe.

In addition to conventional media, we launched an innovative online campaign on NTL's interactive television service, which was its first fully interactive advertising campaign. Under the 'Go Create' slogan a banner ad promoted Sony's AV-IT product range. This enabled the viewer to click on the banner and be taken to a micro-site where they could examine the products in more detail and request further information. Print advertisements were used to identify the specific benefits of individual products in the range.

The whole point behind the different elements of the campaign is to convey an inspirational and invitational attitude which consistently reinforces the fundamental brand promise of new entertainment possibilities through connectivity. The campaign extends beyond advertising to our point-of-sale material, packaging and promotional activity to ensure that our message is always consistent.

'Go Create' is not just an advertising campaign, it is a commitment: Sony is committed to delivering new entertainment opportunities to its consumers through product innovation and ever greater connectivity, combined with on-going education, to ensure our consumers fully understand how our products can be used together.

The 'Go Create' campaign has now been running for nearly a year, and our research has shown that it has had a remarkable effect, not just on the perception of the Sony brand image, but also on consumer attitudes to the digital marketplace. The advertising has significantly increased awareness of the interconnectivity that consumer digital products offer, and as a result the existence of a separate AV-IT market in consumers' minds has been confirmed.

Sony was always seen by the public as the 'King of AV' and therefore as the company 'most likely to succeed' in any new AV-IT market: the 'Go Create' campaign has reinforced this perception across Europe. This in itself is a major success, positioning Sony squarely in pole position just as new competitors seek to enter the AV-IT market.

We are now also seen as a leader in the digital world. The concept of products connecting together to create exciting new entertainment opportunities is becoming more established in the consumer's consciousness, and the European public expects Sony to be at the forefront of the changes they see happening.

The 'Go Create' campaign has played a direct part in achieving this. However, continued product innovation will be necessary in order to further drive positive perceptions of the Sony brand. It is vital that our marketing communications clearly explain to consumers how future innovations will affect their lives, and especially how they will be able to use newly developed Sony products to create yet more opportunities for entertainment and enjoyment.

Commentary

Sony's story is a classic example of the need to define your market carefully – particularly when it is undergoing technological change. Very often, I find companies stick rigidly to traditional market definitions based on historical perspectives of product and geography when they are already outmoded. Particularly in Europe, the history of the nation-state marketing is no longer relevant in many product areas, as similarities between consumer attitudes are now far greater than national differences. So Sony was absolutely right to grasp the nettle of organizational change to break down the boundaries of its previous structure. Its traditional product definitions were increasingly irrelevant to the more sophisticated modern consumer, so without such a change its other efforts could have been negative.

Sony's market position could have been marginalized, as the consumer's attitudes, fired by technology and increasing use of the Internet, diverged from the historic norms.

Sony underpinned its changed definition with some mould-breaking new products and with a brand positioning which occupies the high ground of a generic proposition but which Sony can credibly make its own.

7 | SUNDAY Communications Ltd: New Brand Building Through a Unique Personality

CRAIG EHRLICH, *group managing director*

Outside Hong Kong, few people will have heard of SUNDAY, a mobile telephone provider in the city. Yet despite being launched in only 1997, it now outscores McDonald's and Coke in terms of advertising recall and awareness in Hong Kong. It has had a successful initial public offering (IPO) on the Hong Kong Stock Exchange Main Board and Nasdaq stock markets in March 2000 and recently achieved a positive cash flow. SUNDAY group managing director, Craig Ehrlich, explains.

Brand conception

In 1996, I led a small team in a company named Mandarin Communications, which applied to the Hong Kong Government for the second generation of mobile phone licences. At the time market penetration was in the 20–25 per cent range, mobile phones were an executive accessory primarily owned by businessmen. The market was dominated by major corporate players, largely conglomerates. We expected that the licence application process would also be dominated by major corporates.

From the outset, our licence application and all our internal thinking was based on a number of deep-rooted, inter-related principles: there was a potentially profitable business to be had by moving mobile phones on from the elitist 'just for businessmen' approach to the mainstream – to a mass market of consumers. The way we could do this was by creating a distinctive brand personality and thus a high-profile consumer brand.

Our thinking in doing this was partly influenced by the personal involvement of a number of members of the management team in the creation of Orange. But there were more fundamental reasons than this. We recognized that in the fast-moving and competitive world of mobile telecommunications, we had to be competitive in our technical capability, our coverage and our customer service, but we were unlikely to be superior for long – if at all.

We saw other brands around the world which took on major corporations and created real consumer loyalty through the creation of brand personalities which accurately reflected the needs of contemporary lifestyles. Examples of this were Virgin, the Body Shop and Nike. We saw a gap in the market – certainly in Hong Kong and in the Asian region – for a similar lifestyle brand in mobile phones. We were helped by the very corporatist nature of the marketing of the existing players who largely used celebrity endorsement as their means of promotion – thus continuing the elitist nature of the market proposition. Interestingly we believe that our aspiration to extend the penetration of the market was also attractive to the Hong Kong government and was probably one of the reasons that we won a licence.

Developing the brand values

So having been awarded the licence in 1996 we had just over a year to transform our thoughts into a real brand. At the same time, we had to ensure our service was technically satisfactory and to arrange distribution etc. From the outset, we had a very simple view of our brand values: at its heart, the brand will always challenge the status quo – the essence of our licence application but now with more of an emotional appeal to the consumer. As such it will be irreverent but never rude: this is a fine line, which calls for a lot of judgement. Most importantly our appeal is to the young at heart of all ages – it will be youthful but will not just appeal to the young.

This stems from a fundamental belief that the traditional demographic segmentation of target audiences is increasingly irrelevant in the modern world. My father is in his sixties but still goes jogging in his Nikes – he has more in common with people half his age than with many of his contemporaries. We all know similar examples of people who take up new hobbies or activities late in life which are just as popular amongst people who are twenty or thirty years younger. We also know some twenty- or thirty-year-old couch potatoes who have little empathy with such a lifestyle. So we are a youthful brand with a broad age range of users.

We also recognized that at least at the outset we were a Hong Kong brand and had to reflect the values of the Chinese population. While these values have something in common with city dwellers the world over, we had to recognize the predominately Cantonese culture and ensure we appealed precisely to it. Importantly, though I am an expatriate American, all of our employees are Cantonese.

Inventing the brand

Every famous brand seems to have a quirky story about how its name was invented and ours is no exception.

One of Hong Kong's leading designers was working on our project. The timescale was so short that he had to work over a weekend – his wife was urging him to go shopping with her. He told her she would have to wait until Sunday, the one day of the week Hong Kong people don't work; hence everyone longs for Sunday. He suddenly thought let's call it 'SUNDAY'. 'SUNDAY' means different things to different people, but it conveys feeling of humour, enjoyment and freedom. It's quite simply the day we look forward to the most when we work so hard (when we have time for a family dim sum lunch, friends getting together, a sports game, etc). Although it is an English word, it is easy for Chinese to say and of course many know its meaning.

We also know it would work elsewhere in the region: there was an added benefit as both Hong Kong and Chinese people have very high levels of trust and respect for international brands rather than those which are perceived as purely local.

Making the brand famous

Our prime route for creating our distinctive brand personality has been advertising. Right from the start, when we began our teaser campaign, our ads caused controversy and aroused interest. We were anxious not to let the competition know our chosen name, so we began a teaser campaign which said things like: 'The average male thinks about it twenty times a day', 'You look like you haven't had it in weeks' and 'How many of you are thinking about it right now?' Perhaps fortunately these ads were banned by the Mass Transit Railway for which they were designed and were run in newspapers with 'Banned' stamped across them. Subsequent television ads featured a man breaking wind in front of the Legislative Council building and a woman's breast – with the strapline 'Feels like: SUNDAY'.

Of course this has been a high-cost campaign but we have been fortunate that our major shareholders and our board believed in our brand concept from the beginning. We always knew that the process of creating a truly famous brand was not going to be quick or cheap and so it was not as though we had sprung a surprise on them. We have, of course, had competitor reaction – not least in the form of almost suicidal levels of handset subsidy to new customers.

We have also used promotion and cooperation very extensively. In the early days we used to knock on customers' doors on a Sunday morning with treats and promotional offers (it was a customer loyalty programme) like breakfast on the Peak, or a spicy noodle eating contest where the prize was a trip to Japan, or a swim with local bathing beauties. These really developed a word-of-mouth hum about the brand. We also did a co-promotion with Coca-Cola at their request because they liked our attitude and personality.

We exploited the local obsession with the weather – the Hong

Kong climate changes quite dramatically and suddenly – by sponsoring the local television weather forecast from the Hong Kong Observatory using little filmlets to describe the fifteen or so possible permutations of weather. These short films were a way of reinforcing the brand values everyday and throughout the day while being totally relevant to our target audience.

In 1999, a visit by the award-winning Cirque du Soleil, the Canadian circus, which we partly sponsored, gave us an opportunity to create some totally original and very funky ads all over the subway system, which included decorating trains, platforms, pillars etc. The important thing here was not just that we had created a very visible (and highly talked about) promotion but that we had partnered another organization with the same irreverence and challenge to the norm as our own. It really was a virtuous circle of visibility and consonance of values.

Despite our belief at the outset that we would not be able to innovate technically, we have been the first to utilize location-based technology to beam specific messages to specific customers in specific locations. So if you are, say, eighteen to twenty-five and you enter a particular shopping mall you will be sent an advertisement for one or two stores in that mall which cater for that age range. This is a separate service which now accounts for over 8 per cent of our revenue.

We also changed the way in which the market charged out users by offering unlimited usage for a flat monthly fee during our launch. This did not make the brand famous but it did support the fundamental brand value of challenging the status quo and of reaching out to new customers who might be nervous of the commitment to a conventional billing system.

Managing people

Hong Kong is a difficult market for employers: it has had very low unemployment and staff have become used to being mobile. We also recognized that because of the nature of the brand, and the way in which we operate, we would not suit every potential employee. We have therefore approached recruitment by using similar advertising to our consumer campaign – again challenging the status quo and being irreverent and slightly quirky.

In addition, we have placed a lot of emphasis on managing *all* of our people. For example our stock options went to everyone in the company – including the tea lady. When our share price went down (like everyone in the sector) we were the first company to reissue options at a more realistic price.

We need all of our people to be highly motivated and anxious to support our brand values. I am confident that our organizational structure and remuneration matrix is good, but there is nothing that beats the excitement of working for a really famous and 'hot' brand.

We have, as I mentioned above, also been helped by the stability of our senior management and our original shareholders. There is no doubt in my mind that we could not have achieved what we have without the consistent support of the board. When you are doing something brave and different, the last thing you need is continual questioning of your strategy.

Going public

We used many of the aspects of our branding in the development and communication of our IPO. We created a video and a road-show, which really drew on our brand values and thus the idiosyncrasy of the brand. Somewhat to my surprise this was warmly endorsed by our advisors and the investment community. The communication tools were viewed as some of the best people had seen and, most importantly, investors appreciated what we are trying to do with the brand.

The future

Clearly our first priority is to continue to grow the brand in Hong Kong. We will do this by continued investment in the brand and in service enhancements. The opportunities of technology offered by the third generation of mobile phone licences are immense.

We also believe that SUNDAY has the potential to be a major required brand in South-East Asia where cultural values are similar to those in Hong Kong. Wherever we go the brand will be at the heart of our offer.

Commentary

Brands which seek to develop a distinctive and idiosyncratic personality, with little or no rational underpinning, run some particular risks. Very often, they become an excuse for self-indulgent advertising that wins awards but fails to motivate. On the other hand in a world of media saturation a distinctive or even quirky idea can bring rewards of awareness saliency and personal identification with the brand personality.

This is the trick SUNDAY has successfully pulled off, helped by the ability to capture the particular psyche of the Hong Kong Chinese. It is not a recipe for every brand and I generally prefer at least some rational promise.

SUNDAY is noteworthy too for making sure every part of its marketing mix supports the distinctive brand personality. Often creative and unusual advertising lacks support and similar deftness in promotions, sponsorship and PR.

8 | Visa International: The Serendipity of a Name

MALCOLM WILLIAMSON, CEO, *and*
CAROLINE B. McNALLY, *executive vice president,*
global brand management

By all measures Visa has been a global success story. It has more share –
about 60 per cent – of global payment card volume than all other payment
systems combined. Its ratings in consumer preference surveys are consist-
ently double those of its nearest competitor. And it always ranks very high
in top global brand studies. Yet like any world class brand, Visa cannot
afford to rest on its laurels. Visa faces new competition in a changing
payment services industry. New technologies, channels of commerce and
new and nimble players have toppled leaders in other industries. As part
of its strategy to defend itself against these challenges, Visa has increased
its commitment to protecting and building the Visa brand. Its CEO and
its executive vice president of global brand management discuss their efforts
to extend Visa's powerful brand to meet the demands of the future economy.

A new, more strategic focus on brand

Visa International is firmly committed to the idea that in the
age of multi-channel commerce a strong brand could well end up
being a corporation's most important asset – potentially more
valuable than any other item on the balance sheet. Of course
revenue and profit streams, distribution networks, management
expertise and intellectual property will remain important, but we
believe that only a strong brand will allow their full value to be
realized.

Visa has focused on building its brand globally since its inception,
but in 1995 we embarked on a deliberate strategy of brand

expansion. This was a conscious decision to put our brand strategy to work in support of our corporate strategic objectives. There are some interesting lessons in the story of why we adopted this goal, the approach we took, and what we learnt in applying the approach to different new businesses.

The serendipity of a name

Visa, as a privately held association of 21,000 member banks around the world, has an unusual corporate branding challenge. The Visa brand works in partnership with our members' brands, contributing specific values and providing them with international reach. For many members the ability to globally utilize this brand, which is among the world's most widely recognized and respected, is one of the most important benefits of their association with Visa. As the stewards of the Visa brand, we believe that we can take some credit for its successes, but it can't be denied that we are blessed by fortune in the name Visa.

It was not always this way. The original brand, launched in 1958, was BankAmericard. NBI (National BankAmericard Incorporated) purchased the blue, white and gold bands and the name from the Bank of America, which was then a leading regional bank in the US, and proceeded to build a global system. Since BankAmericard didn't play too well outside the western United States, NBI's member banks adopted various other names around the world that were generally based on their name, for example, the Sumitomo Card in Japan and Barclaycard in the UK. Although these cards shared the colour bands, in 1973 NBI realized that the lack of a common name was hindering growth. NBI's then president, Dee Hock, was known for his entrepreneurial style. Consistent with his independent views, Dee took a direct approach to developing a new name and invited the entire staff to participate. It was agreed that the name should be culturally and geographically neutral, have no restrictive connotations, and imply mobility, acceptance and travel. He offered a challenge and a reward to the person submitting the selected name – $50! Notwithstanding the reward, a frenzy of brainstorming ensued.

As the story goes, the final choice was made in a conference room with twelve staff members around the table. Beginning with forty potential names they quickly eliminated many. From the shortlist of five, Visa was the unanimous choice. As the next few years showed, this choice was unquestionably one of the most important in Visa's history. From 1975 to 1980 Visa's sales more than tripled. The name was a powerful magnet; many banks switched all their cards to Visa and card issuance mushroomed. Time has proven that the values they sought in the name are indeed evoked in the minds of consumers when they hear the name Visa.

Is brand really important?

This experience of great success following on the change to a common name gave us abundant evidence that the brand mattered, that for Visa it played a key role both in banks' and consumers' choices and helped support the promise of global functionality. Yet in recent years various marketing pundits have predicted the death of brand as a critical factor in the new economy. Certainly some established brands have lost their position to upstarts.

So why are we so strongly convinced that brands are becoming more important, not less? In our world of rapid technological change, we see products introduced at an unparalleled rate, features and prices are copied just as quickly and the first mover advantage is shrinking. Consumers face an extraordinary range of choice and are often overwhelmed with information. In this environment, brands provide help in making choices; they offer 'a short cut' as consumers tend to gravitate to brands they can trust. It is clear, for example, that a new brand in the payment arena would have to make significant investments in time, money and effort to build the trust that is the core of Visa's promise and has been established over the past three decades. This is even more true when we look to arenas of commerce such as the Internet which, because they are new and unproven, raise anxiety for many consumers.

We believe that it is strong, positive customer experiences that create this kind of trust and thus build sustainable marketplace advantage. It is said that a brand is a promise of value to customers. More than ever then, a *strong brand* will represent a *credible promise* sustained over time. Today, for a global company, the promise must also be universal. It can't break down over the oceans. Consumers are too mobile, markets too closely linked and the Internet too pervasive.

Adopting a strategy of brand expansion

In 1994–95, Visa undertook a major assessment of corporate strategy. We faced major new challenges, particularly in the realms of new technologies, new competitors, new channels of commerce and greater diversity in the needs of our members. As we considered how best to ensure future growth and profitability, we assessed our strengths – global transaction processing systems, information technology, operations, product development, and the Visa brand. As a corporation we needed to build on all these strengths.

Historically marketing and brand strategy had been quite separate activities at Visa – they were not fully integrated with corporate strategy. Visa was, and still to a great extent is, a systems-oriented culture: this is due both to operational imperatives and to the fact that our member banks are the actual card issuers and as such own the customer relationship. To the vast majority of our staff, our customers are our member banks: it is the banks' customers who are the consumers that carry the Visa card. Yet, we felt that we could and should capitalize more on the Visa brand given its global potential and belief in the increasing importance of brands in the emerging marketplace. In 1995, a *Fortune* survey of global CEOs rated Visa as one of the world's top ten best managed brands, and we had rated near the top in Interbrand's World's Top Brands study. We had a position of strength to build from. We wanted to find a way for brand strategy to play a direct role in supporting, even driving, corporate strategy.

We set out to do a full assessment and benchmarking of the Visa brand globally. There was a short list of key strategic questions we wanted to answer. These included: what equities does the Visa brand own, functionally and emotionally? How is the brand differentiated from both traditional and emerging competitors' brands? What are the permissions that the brand has and what are the constraints? How elastic is the brand?

We learnt a number of enormously valuable things from this process. We confirmed what we had believed, that Visa is indeed perceived as a global or universal brand. Better than that, we learnt that all over the world people also believe Visa is local and prefer it for that reason. Of course, the connection to their own bank is critical, but repeatedly we also heard comments like: 'I use Visa because it is French.'

The key attributes associated with Visa in consumers' minds were very consistent around the world and included both functional and emotional benefits: convenience, reliability/trustworthiness, safety and security are attributes that consumers associate with the brand. It is also seen as versatile – 'for people like me'. We also learned that the Visa brand stood for *single-product* functionality in consumers' minds – that is, depending on the country in which they lived, it meant it was seen as either a credit or a debit facility. At the same time, consumers clearly had the expectation that Visa could be more than it was. The opportunity for brand extension behind a strong marketing programme was clearly ours to capture.

At that time, we had a lot of product development and information technology people generating many new business ideas that they wanted to put the Visa name on. As we looked at these opportunities to expand our business, key questions for the corporation were: should we have a multi-brand strategy, or should we extend the Visa brand? We understood that brands expand only with the permission of their public. So, given the equities we had identified in the Visa brand, we asked just how far we could go with new products and services before we would disconnect with our consumers.

Our research suggested that the Visa brand equities clearly had reached within the realm of 'payment'. We concluded that a strategy of expanding the meaning of the Visa brand to encompass more ways to pay – debit, stored value, electronic payments, etc. – was the best way to effectively marshall the brand's power, in addition to our other strengths, in support of corporate strategy. We determined that, under the umbrella of the Visa brand, our association should strive to become the 'world's best way to pay.'

Building a brand culture

We set about creating a brand culture within Visa. We wanted all of our employees to think about 'brand first' – to make business decisions considering the strength of the brand and how it can work for us. Of course, not every corporate strategic decision is made solely considering the criterion of capitalizing on and building the brand, but this perspective has powerfully influenced our direction in many situations. For example, a key decision that Visa made was *not* to capitalize on our transaction 'railroad' to capture non-Visa branded volume.

Reinforcing brand awareness is a continual challenge at Visa. From the brand management perspective, we see that though we talk brand first, we don't always behave in ways that reflect that goal. One of our continuing internal struggles is between our capacity – what we *can* do – and what it is right for the brand to do. It is often difficult and not always desirable to restrain the enthusiasm of our technical groups for new and perhaps tangential opportunities. We try to find a balance between openness to potential new directions and focus on existing priorities.

Also, the reality is that our member banks are ultimately the distribution system – they are really the front line to the customers. And their priority, of course, is to differentiate their own brand in the market, rather than to reinforce Visa's. We work closely with them to try and ensure that the Visa brand retains and builds on its core values while contributing the equities of additional confidence and global acceptance to their brands. In our product development efforts we constantly seek to provide members with options that will support their own strategic business goals while pursuing our goal of taking Visa into new payment arenas.

Implementing brand expansion – some case examples

Some case examples help illustrate the way we are implementing our brand expansion strategy. These programmes represent different scenarios: Electron was an existing, stand-alone acceptance platform that we decided to bring under the corporate brand umbrella, while Visa Cash was a brand new stored-value payment technology. As in most areas of business, the things we decided not to do may be as important as those that we did. The Visa Cash story includes an opportunity we chose not to pursue. It also provides another example of a *no* decision with respect to the Visa brand.

Visa Electron

The Electron acceptance mark was introduced in Europe and Latin America in the early nineties. Banks there needed a system to lower risk, enabling payment card options for market segments with a limited credit history. To minimize the risk, every transaction had to be authorized, but at that time 100 per cent authorization was not the rule outside the US. Since the Visa flag mark at a merchant point of sale stands for universal acceptance (i.e., that all Visa-flagged cards are accepted), a different acceptance mark was needed to distinguish merchant locations, which were electronic and offered online authorization. This was the rationale for the introduction of Electron as a new acceptance mark without Visa branding.

As we looked at our brand assessment results, we asked the question of whether it made sense to maintain Electron separately or to begin diversifying Visa. In this case, the basic options explored were endorsement ('Electron from Visa') or sub-branding ('Visa Electron'). We decided on sub-branding. Since it could be used on either a debit or credit card Electron fit within the existing meaning of Visa; by making it Visa Electron, research suggested we could transfer the values of Visa to Electron. Of course, we recognized that this decision carried with it some risks as sub-branding inevitably does, and we are constantly vigilant to ensure that the core promise and meaning of the brand and the Visa flag is not damaged.

The impact of the name change to Visa Electron was significant in terms of increased member issuance and product roll-out. The acceptance mark became much easier to sell to members: the Visa name added credibility and desirability. In addition to the name, we still had to resolve the specific design of the acceptance mark to reference Visa equities but to avoid confusion. The solution we found and some of the dilemmas it raised are discussed below in the section on the role of visual identity.

Visa Cash
The second example came shortly after we committed to the Visa brand expansion strategy, and this time it was a new payment technology, stored value. This was our first opportunity to move into a new 'way to pay'. We had developed a stored-value product with all the associated issuance and acceptance infrastructure. Unlike the previous examples, this one was distinctly new and totally different from any previous Visa products. It would indeed expand the brand's reach.

At the same time there were voices that argued we should utilize the technology as a platform by licensing it broadly for use by non-Visa products. It was at that point that we made a strategic decision to reserve the technology for our own brand expansion. Of course, this conflict will go away as common standards are developed for stored-value products, but at the time it was an important decision on how to focus our energies.

Having made the decision to move forward with a strictly branded product, we selected the name Visa Cash. We faced a similar challenge, as with Electron, of indicating to consumers where they could find this unique kind of acceptance, the best and most tangible example of which is a vending machine. Also, as with Electron, we developed an acceptance mark that takes advantage of the Visa logo but is distinct from the traditional flag. The stored-value payment category is still relatively small, so we can't point to great success yet. Nevertheless, we believe that the branding decision is right and that Visa Cash will contribute to our goal of making Visa the 'world's best way to pay'.

We mentioned earlier the importance of decisions *not* to pursue opportunities. Just as we decided not to license our technology to support a generic 'my brand cash' product, we also decided not to link the Visa brand to the Plus brand. Plus is an ATM-only mark which Visa acquired to add to its debit transaction processing capabilities. Just as we considered Visa branding for Electron, we also looked at the question for Plus. However, the Plus network supports many brands and we concluded that the reach would be too great for consumers and also that the potential benefit of the Visa name was limited. Accordingly Plus remains as a stand-alone unlinked brand within Visa.

The two case studies summarized here have helped move Visa away from being only a credit/or only a debit card brand. Our challenges now mostly lie in the area beyond cards – as we look to the future we must ensure that our brand thrives in the virtual world of e-payment.

The role of visual identity in supporting our brand expansion strategy

Perhaps more than for most other companies, visual identity is a critical component of the Visa brand. The Visa flag and various other marks do not signify products; they signify acceptance, and universal acceptance is absolutely one of the core values of the brand. The flag in particular stands for our core promise to our cardholders – wherever you see the flag you can use your Visa card.

When we decided on a strategy of brand expansion, we were obviously conscious of the need to protect our brand identity and marks. As part of understanding what the Visa brand means to consumers all over the world, we also undertook identity research. We learned that the original Visa flag with the blue, white and gold bands, while most universally recognized, is strongly associated in consumers' minds with the original product and definitely stands for ubiquitous acceptance. In this sense, it was somewhat limiting for new products.

When we moved into new areas, like stored value, with Visa Cash, we found that by associating the flag with them we risked disenfranchising our core customer by not meeting our core promise of ubiquitous acceptance. In our testing, we tried the flag with the word 'cash' on it; people assumed that any card with the flag on it could be used there. Maintaining the 100 per cent acceptance promise of the flag was widely accepted as critical to our brand stewardship.

Thus we faced an important challenge in sub-branding. We needed to find a way of showing acceptance for these new products that would be distinct, still providing a Visa halo, but not harming the meaning of the Visa flag. We ultimately developed an evolution of our Visa word mark, enhancing it with the comet to serve as exclamatory punctuation. Research indicated that the Visa word mark was the single most recognized element of the Visa identity so we decided to use it as the core element in extending our branding system.

The enhanced word mark, when combined with another word and shown in a blue box, proved to have several advantages for sub-branding. First, because the Visa word mark was widely known people generally understood that it was Visa. At the same time, separating it from the flag made it distinct enough to minimize the confusion. After all, the current point of sale system is based on matching marks. When consumers see the sign in a shop they compare it with their card and if the marks match they expect it to work. The new acceptance marks for Visa Electron and Visa Cash are different enough so that most people are not too confused (see the following illustration).

Figure 5: Visa acceptance marks - flag, Visa Cash and Visa Electron

It should be noted, however, that in the US the decision was made not to use the Visa Electron mark – in part because research there indicated it did generate confusion. Since Visa Electron is not issued in the US market, it was felt that the possible negatives related to brand confusion outweighed the need to use the mark.

A third advantage of the new design is that consumers associate the comet image with attributes such as modernity, innovation and technological advance, all of which are things that came out with somewhat lower ratings in the core Visa brand research. We believe that adding these attributes to the brand over time will help carry us forward.

Also, looking to the not so distant future, we recognize that our brand will no longer live only on plastic. When the 'point of sale' may be a PC, cell phone or PDA, we have made it a priority to develop new forms of brand expression, new ways of signaling that Visa is accepted for payment. We have recently adopted a new animated logo with a unique sound to extend the brand in e-commerce, mobile commerce and other emerging forms of payment beyond the point of sale. Our goal with these new forms of 'identity' is to make it convenient, trustworthy and comfortable for consumers to pay with Visa whether or not there is a card to swipe. We want the audio and animation to signal to our users that they can expect the same high level of convenience and security that a Visa product provides in the physical world and therefore that Visa is the best payment choice in the virtual world as well as in the physical one.

In short, to support our brand expansion strategy our goal has been to develop and implement a visual identity system that makes it easy for consumers to understand which Visa product can be used where. We want people to always be able to pay with Visa. Yet, as the payment environments and payment types diversify, we recognize that not all Visa products will work in all locations. As we look to the future we hope ultimately to be able to put as many products as possible under the flag – to offer universal acceptance with expanded payment functionality.

In 1995 the Visa flag basically stood for single product functionality and acceptance. Our vision is that the flag will come to stand for payment – all kinds of payment – as well as for acceptance. Ironically one of the future goals might be that some of the new marks we've created will actually go away over time as the technologies evolve to support inter-operability across products.

For Visa the past decade has been a time of growing recognition of the value of our brand – and of what an important role brand strategy can play in supporting corporate strategy. As champions of the brand we have also gained a greater appreciation for the responsibility we have to preserve, strengthen and expand our brand rather than take it for granted. As they say about aging brains and muscles, 'use it or lose it'. Similarly, if you wish to preserve the relevance of your brand promise to your consumers, you must make the effort to understand and respond to their expectations for growth and evolution. A static brand promise is a dying brand.

Commentary

The global development of Visa is interesting for me in two respects. The ability to develop brands on a global yet local business level is a vivid example of Theodore Levitt's famous saying: 'Think global: act local'. Indeed it is fascinating to see that Visa is perceived as a local brand in many countries, while clearly also having the authority and cachet of a global brand. This, combined with its outstanding levels of trust and dependability, shows the value and strength of long-term consistent branding.

Secondly, Visa demonstrates that powerful brands are capable of extension into adjacent areas, without diluting the core brand. This sort of work is never easy and requires a detailed understanding of the brand values in order to both assess the ability to stretch and to protect their integrity.

9 | Vodafone: Post-Aquisition: The Challenge of Brand Migration

CHRIS GENT, *chief executive*

Vodafone has been transformed from a predominantly UK-based company into the largest mobile phone company and one of the largest companies (by market capitalization) in the world through a series of substantial acquisitions. This has raised important aspects of branding and marketing described here by chief executive, Chris Gent.

The strategic context

When I became chief executive of Vodafone in 1997, we were already established as the market leader in the UK and had some presence overseas, notably in Australia and some minority stakes in other markets. We had relationships with overseas cellular phone operators in order to provide access for our customers in those countries. However, in general the global market for mobile telephony was organized on largely national lines (like the fixed-wire market). But there were signs that this was changing and I commissioned a strategic review to assess the international market.

From a technical standpoint, the spectrum, speed and capacity of the technical standards for the new generation services would satisfy the demand for all voice traffic and enable wireless to be substituted for fixed-line capacity for consumers. The new technical standards would also enable a whole range of new non-voice services for both businesses and the individual. This included the potential for making a reality of Internet access and other data services for wireless users.

In addition, the process of international standardization, which had already occurred with global systems for mobile communication (GSM), would be extended with the third generation of mobile phone licences so that we could envisage world service provision with new applications and products, particularly in the data field, which would give advantage to the global player. This would extend the advantage of international roaming which was already available through GSM.

These two capabilities when combined with a global presence would enable a globally competent and capable operator to differentiate their services for the corporate user, which are generally the most profitable, as well as optimizing their position with the higher spending and increasingly internationally mobile consumer market.

In Europe it was clear that demand for mobile communications showed no signs of slowing and had made a breakthrough in popular culture. It had changed the way people conducted their lives and was a highly desired service. In some respects this phenomenon is only now happening in the US.

Our strategic analysis also showed that the major fixed-wire telecoms companies – many fairly recently privatized – had ambitions to grow beyond their national boundaries. The next generation of mobile phone licences were not far away and this would provide them and others with a potential means of entry. Although we did not know at that time that they would largely follow the UK model of an auction, we knew that such licences would not come cheap.

We sensed a changing marketplace in which there would be only a few really successful global players, who would require access to capital markets and strong on-going cash flow in order to be able to purchase the new licences, invest in research and development, maintain their infrastructure and continue with appropriate investment in marketing, in order to maintain customer loyalty and to recruit new customers.

We identified significant synergies in this changed scenario, particularly in procurement and in research and development. In procurement we would be able to use our buying power to reduce the cost of equipment purchase, and in R&D there was plainly a huge amount of duplicated effort in developing and introducing new services. We identified some possible synergies in marketing but recognized that this area would require much more detailed work before they could be accurately quantified.

We therefore embarked upon a three-pronged growth strategy. First we aimed to become a global business so that we could optimize services to customers and differentiate ourselves from regional and national players. Secondly we decided to accelerate growth in our existing markets, through the active promotion of prepay products aimed at the customer, through investment both in our marketing capability with our own retail outlets and in non-specialist multiple retailers. We also consolidated and developed our brand identity in each of our territories. Finally we determined to work on non-voice services, which, though we knew would take time to develop, would eventually provide sustained growth and enhance margins as Vodafone moved up the value chain.

To achieve our ambition to become a global player we evaluated a number of options. In some cases our partners were not in cellular phones as a core business but were hoping to enjoy a good investment return when they exited. This enabled us to gain control in places like the Netherlands and Greece. We were also successful in bidding for new licences in countries such as Egypt and in making individual country acquisitions such as in New Zealand.

However, to become a true global player needed major moves and this is the strategic context of the two large acquisitions undertaken by Vodafone in the space of less than a year. The first acquisition was AirTouch, a significant cellular phone operator on the west coast of the US with the added benefit of a number of stakes in mobile phone companies in Europe. This was an agreed deal, albeit in the face of stiff competition from Bell Atlantic on the east coast of the US. Subsequently we combined with Bell Atlantic and the wireless interests of GTE to create the leading operator in the US with over 23 million customers, a single digital technical standard and a presence in forty-nine out of the fifty markets. This gave the combined entity a nationally branded offering to retain and win the highest spending customers through a pan-US presence.

Soon after the completion of this transaction, Hutchinson Whampoa, the owner of Orange, a major UK competitor with some presence in other markets, sold its shareholding to Mannesmann, a German conglomerate, with interests in both fixed-wire and cellular phones. More importantly, Mannesmann had been a partner with AirTouch for some years and the two companies had shareholdings in mobile phone companies elsewhere in Europe. We simply could not stand back and allow our European infrastructure to be taken over by a competitor, but more importantly our work on synergies gave us, and ultimately our shareholders, the confidence to press on with the first contested bid in German history. This is not the place to dwell in detail on that battle but eventually we prevailed and in early 2000 took control of Mannesmann. However it was clear that as around 70 per cent of Mannesmann's shareholders were outside Germany and 40 per cent were also Vodafone shareholders their acceptance of an all-paper share offer was an endorsement of our global strategy.

The groundwork for a branding strategy

As I said earlier, we had done some initial work on the possible marketing synergies from the enlarged business but recognized that we needed a more detailed appraisal. The enlarged group had subsidiaries in all the major countries in Europe, in the US and in a number of other markets. All had different names, different profiles, different product mixes and different histories. The battle for Mannesmann had left some bruised egos, particularly in Germany, where there were some lingering concerns that the British were about to ride roughshod over their brand heritage and positioning.

We immediately approached brand consultants Springpoint, who had been invaluable in managing the brand repositioning project, to assist us in this work. They undertook a major research programme in all our major markets to understand the existing brand franchise and positioning in each market.

As is usual when multinational research is undertaken, every country management team was anxious to point out the unique features of their market or their business. Springpoint was helpful in focusing everyone on the similarities between countries, not the differences. In fact these similarities were substantial and fundamental, primarily due to the market structure. Across Europe governments had allowed their own post office telecom (PT) to be either the first or joint first cellular phone company. This had led to a market structure where the old PT business was the safe, steady company and our brand was seen as the 'challenger' brand offering perceptions of modernity, freedom and innovation. This was at its height in Italy, where the old state-run PT was hugely inefficient, leading to high penetration of mobile phones and a very weak brand image for its own cellular phone brand. Our company, Omnitel, had an outstanding brand image with a reputation of service and innovation. Most of our other companies also had strong brand images, with a similar vocabulary, albeit less powerfully expressed. All the brands in our portfolio were number one or two in their respective markets, so there were no weak links.

Our home market in the UK had a very different structure since BT had only entered the market as a minority partner in a joint venture and Vodafone was seen by many as the safe, authoritative brand, with Orange and One-2-One, the more recent entrants, as the challenger brands. In part this was for reasons of history and in part because we had deliberately built a strong franchise in the corporate segment of the market where we found, historically, greater brand loyalty and higher usage.

It was also clear that, because mobile telephony is a new young market, consumers expected change. They had seen massive innovation in terms of physical product, new services being introduced, new payment methods and new entrants. Many saw mergers, takeovers and alliances as part of everyday life. At the same time it was also apparent that the mobile phone had become for most users an indispensable part of their everyday lifestyle: it was something that they could not do without. Some quotations bring this to life:

'I couldn't cope without it.'

'I don't know how I ever managed before.'

'What do I always keep in my handbag? My lipstick, my credit cards and my phone.'

This was a pivotal moment in the development of the brand. We needed to consider very carefully how to go forward. We explored attitudes of our management in each country as well as the consumer, since they would be responsible for implementing our strategy. Here again we found some degree of similarity. The bruises of the battle for Mannesman left some degree of suspicion of the corporate management and their intentions, as might be expected. They also saw change as a constant feature of their market, so a change of ownership was but another change they had to manage. Perhaps more importantly, our local management were fiercely proud of their local brands. In many cases they had been there from the beginning, joining a small risky venture in its early days and having consequently a feeling of parental responsibility for the baby they had nurtured. In a number of countries they described their battle with the established giant PT company as 'David versus Goliath'. As one manager said:

We changed the shape of this industry . . . we made a huge number of innovations in marketing, products, services, technology. We made it possible for everybody to buy a cellphone, which wasn't possible when the market was dominated by a state owned giant. And the people in the company are proud of that and proud to work for the company.

Our managers could see the advantage for stronger links between the companies although preferably without making any change to the brand name. They saw enormous benefits coming from the new links with Vodafone: they immediately identified advantages from combined purchasing power, transfer of best practice, representation of regulatory authorities, the creation of global products and services and the development of their and their colleagues' careers. And all the companies had a strong customer ethos and prided themselves on their dynamism, service, efficiency and innovation. There were some concerns that the entrepreneurial spirit and the vigour of the organization could be lost in a multinational giant. There was a perceived risk of losing customers and high-calibre personnel in the local team.

So we had a starting point for developing a European strategy at least, without a clear consensus of where to go.

The case for a single brand

As one might expect from the attitudes of local managers expressed above, there was no overwhelming desire for local name changes. They had worked hard and invested money in developing a local brand equity and saw no point in 'throwing this away'. All the other synergy benefits did not require common branding, so why not focus on achieving those and why risk the change?

I understand this attitude, although I do not agree with it. We clearly had some very similar brand positionings around Europe and so we were not trying to unite totally different brand franchises. More importantly we looked hard at the future development of the market and attitudes of consumers. It is clear that the core benefits of mobile phones are universal – the opportunity and freedom to communicate when and where you want. These benefits do not fundamentally differ from Milan to Malmo or Manchester to Malaga. Of course there will be higher usage in countries with poor fixed-line networks and a different product mix between business and consumer and between pay as you go and conventional billing, but the basic benefit is the same.

The introduction of WAP technology will begin to change this: it will no longer be just voice communication for the majority and data communication for some business users, but it will provide totally mobile access to Internet content and to transactions on the Net. Thus, the emotional benefit, which it was believed that we could legitimately own, was the offer of 'a richer and more fulfilling life'. But, like to many promises, this was generic to the sector and would be mere hot air without some solid and differentiating substantiation.

One key factor in evaluating this was the attitude of consumers themselves to a single brand: most of the attitudes were positive – more innovation, new and better services – but there were some lingering concerns – would prices increase, would local services be reduced to a lowest common denominator, would local customer service deteriorate? We felt we could address all these issues in one way or another since it would never be our intention to tamper with local service if it was working well and we would add new services and values. One other critical factor was that users of mobile phones, and particularly heavy users, travel a great deal and see the current roaming capability as a highly desirable benefit. You only have to watch a business flight disembark at any airport to have vivid empirical evidence of this. However roaming as currently configured is not ideal since not all features are available and some-times they need different numbers for access. A key product advan-tage would be our ability to offer identical services with identical numbers anywhere in the world.

We had already taken the decision to form a joint venture with the giant French media company Vivendi for the entertainment content of our core Internet offer. We judged that the quality of this offer would be greatly enhanced by more resources and a larger customer base than if Vodafone went ahead alone. For other input, notably our sport and business offer on the Internet, we judged that greater local tailoring would be required and we will be provid-ing this ourselves.

We therefore came to the conclusion that we could provide some real substantiation to the brand positioning which fitted our brand profile and our customers needs. We also judged that over time we would have the resources and imagination to develop new services for our customers to provide on-going justification for our claims.

Vodafone itself was largely unknown except in Germany, where the profile of the bid battle meant that everyone had heard of us. Interestingly now the heat of that battle had died down there were no significant negatives associated with the brand. We also explored attitudes to the British/English provenance of Vodafone. In northern Europe, British companies are seen as more likely to be sensitive to local culture than others might be but are not considered to be as technically advanced as German companies. There is some feeling there that we are not good Europeans and will only speak English! By contrast in southern Europe, Britishness implies reliability, trustworthiness, punctuality, flexibility and sensitivity to other cultures as well as more advanced technology. Overall there is an acceptance of the existence of multinational companies in the modern world and the feeling that mobile telecommunications was an industry in which one would expect multinationals to exist.

There were a number of other important factors which swayed our decision. Historically international marketing was largely about shared advertising and certainly satellite television and the Net make this an important factor. On the other hand it is a very limiting perspective on the modern marketing mix. Vodafone in the UK has invested heavily, and successfully, in sponsorship – initially of cricket and horseracing, but latterly with sponsorship of Manchester United, one of the most widely followed football clubs in the world. We see sponsorship as a means of both maintaining brand saliency through continuous media coverage of our corporate identity and building our relationship with our business customers and suppliers through high-quality corporate entertainment. Clearly I do not expect the mass of our European customers to receive much coverage of the English cricket squad or even of the Derby! (Although both have had spin off benefits in South Africa, New Zealand and Australia.) However our relationship with Manchester United has a global dimension – we are already getting mentions of the Vodafone connection with the team in our market research in continental Europe – and there may also be opportunities for major international sport sponsorship in the future. It is much easier to consider this with a single brand.

The process of acquiring both AirTouch and Mannesman had given us a huge profile in the investment community, amongst both professionals and private investors. We have moved to being the largest company by capitalization in the UK and one of the top five in the world. As a result Vodafone was a name on every investors lips. I believe it is right that we seek to reinforce this by maintaining the link between the corporate brand and its key operating constituents.

Finally, the competition authorities in Brussels imposed a condition for their approval of our acquisitions of Mannesmann that we must divest its shareholding in Orange. While we initially considered a flotation, we eventually concluded that, if we could achieve the right price, a trade sale could deliver an advantage of speed and equivalent if not superior value. We eventually sold Orange to France Telecom for £31 billion. In doing so, we recognized that we were creating a bigger competitor and that the enlarged entity would move forward rapidly with the Orange name. This meant that there was likely to be at least one other international rival with the advantage of a single brand name and positioning. I felt that we would not risk compromise for Vodafone in the light of such competition.

Implementing a single brand

We therefore reached the conclusion that we should move forward with a single global brand. Further work on the potential synergies in marketing revealed that significant savings could be achieved. Even if these were not delivered completely, the sums involved were sufficiently large to prevent any serious discussion of maintaining the status quo. The company operates in an international, technology-based market and perceptions of technology brands are enhanced if they are believed to be multinational. Consumers have an instinctive grasp of the benefits of scale in technology. Our customers are highly mobile and use our product all over the world for both business and leisure purposes. There remained the challenge of how to transfer the equity from the local brands to the global brand.

The decision was also made that the brand should be Vodafone.

Inevitably, the act of compressing many months of work and a huge volume of market research might make this sound a clear-cut decision: while it was clearly my preference and that of my colleagues in corporate management, we believed it wrong to impose it unilaterally. There was some consideration of a totally new brand name or the adoption of one of the existing brands in the portfolio. However, since Vodafone was well established in the UK and a number of other markets, accounting for over 20 per cent of revenues, it seemed wasteful to invest in creating and promoting a new brand name in the absence of any significant negatives and with some positive factors mentioned above.

In any event, we clearly had to devise a transition strategy since we could not build Rome/Vodafone in a day. Again we used Springpoint to assist us, particularly in developing the final brand positioning and the design architecture of the transitional approach. We set up a steering group with representatives from a number of different countries and the corporate centre. We wanted to tap into the local entrepreneurial spirit and creativity. I believe that much damage can be done by forcing through this sort of change in an imperialistic way. We are aiming for an organizational structure that will facilitate local execution within an agreed framework in a timely fashion – without the need for a costly central bureaucracy to control everything. At the same time we put in place structures and mechanisms to stimulate the realization of some of the benefits of the enlarged Group – cross-fertilization of ideas, exchange of best practice, generation of new products and services, career development and opportunities for secondment to other markets or to the corporate centre.

As our brand positioning developed, we consciously sought to take some common values that exist across all the brands in our portfolio and some values that are salient only in some countries. In particular, although Vodafone is strongest in the UK and, of course, our corporate headquarters are based there, we wanted to avoid falling into the trap of imposing a British brand based on our British values. Vodafone in the future must be seen as a true global brand, with no home territory, yet clearly in touch with local cultures in the markets where it operates. We have deliberately set up our headquarters of our European marketing operation in Dusseldorf, a continual reminder that we are building a global, not a British brand. The brand will need to capture the hearts and minds of our customers and our employees. We must not be seen as an everyday commodity but as a truly inspirational brand.

The core positioning is that Vodafone enables people to get more out of life. We see this in two ways:

- as fulfilling – opening up more possibilities so you can do more of what you want to do
- as empowering – giving you control so you can live your life the way you want to and connect with the communities that are important to you.

We support this with a number of important underlying core values:

Dependability
Empathy
Can-do attitude
Innovation
Joie de vivre

There was a clear need for a migration strategy in order to transfer the undoubted equity in the local brands to Vodafone in a timely and effective way. This will require an interim dual-branding phase with the local brand and Vodafone appearing together for anything from six months to two years. However we recognized that the brand identity itself is only one part of the equation: elements such as new product development and continuity of service as well as other internal and external communication will all be crucial to the transfer of equity. Somewhat unusually, we established the principle that, during the transition phase, the local brand will be dominant with Vodafone as a lower level endorsement, along with some local freedom to decide on the right framework for the presentation of the two brand identities.

As I write this in late 2000, the new positioning and the transitional branding identity are poised for introduction early next year. We now have operations in twenty-five countries, across five continents, serving 65 million customers. We still have places in the world where we would like to be, notably in South-East Asia and Latin America. I am confident that we will be able to make Vodafone a powerful global consumer brand with high levels of awareness and strong emotional values in a short space of time. I am also excited by the prospect of enabling the brand to be an inspirational symbol for the dynamism and enthusiasm of our workforce worldwide.

Commentary

I have to declare an interest here since I was personally involved in the work for Vodafone at Springpoint. As a result I could easily make this conclusion as long as the chapter! However, for me the first key point to the Vodafone story is the need to manage the post-acquisition process in a way that recognizes the sensitivities of individuals and, perhaps more importantly, the potential contribution of the acquired companies. All too often macho management seeks to impose its wisdom on a company whereas the reality is that there is much to be contributed to the acquirer by new insights, different experiences, better services and so on. Additionally it is important that the brand values (and for that matter the cultural values) of the enlarged organization draw on the best of everyone – not just what the acquirer has been doing.

The second point is that acquisitions are frequently a stimulus for organizational and cultural change as well as branding alignment but that branding is a critical means of ensuring the other changes happen. In other words, it is the requirement to embrace and endorse a set of explicit brand values by everyone that provides the catalyst for fundamental change within the whole organization. Branding has huge internal value to any organization as well as its traditional external role to the businesses' competitors and customers.

10 | Vorwerk: Building a Brand Without Media Advertising

ACHIM SCHWANITZ, *managing partner*

The spiralling cost of media promotion is a long-standing gripe amongst marketers. One company has managed to achieve brand leadership, powerful brand values and strong awareness without spending a penny on conventional advertising. Here Achim Schwanitz, managing partner of Vorwerk, explains his company's strategy.

Vorwerk is a privately owned company based in Wuppertal, Germany. A growing proportion of its sales are in other countries so that now over half its turnover is outside Germany. The main engines of its international growth have been two distinctive products: a unique vacuum cleaner specially designed for thorough cleaning deep down and a unique kitchen appliance, which prepares and cooks food.

These products are not available through retail outlets but only via direct sales, using a network of trained sales advisers, who present the products in customers' homes. Vorwerk has employed this sales method for over 70 years. The products are unique and have strong in-built benefits, which are most powerfully communicated by in-home demonstration. This personal contact results in the high brand value of our products. Without any conventional advertising, we promote our products by demonstrations in the customers' own homes and by superior quality which speaks for itself.

Core drivers of the Vorwerk brand

Vorwerk has superior products. Both the Kobold (vacuum cleaner) and Thermomix (which prepares and cooks food) have high performance when compared to products sold in retail outlets, and both are marked by unique features. The Kobold has built on its historical technical platform, of high vacuum power with very small dimensions, to include the most modern filter technology available – which is of significant benefit to those allergic to dust. For example, the Kobold is not only a typical vacuum cleaner, but also a core appliance, which can be both an upright hand-held-machine or a floor cleaner. Using several connecting devices, the Kobold satisfies customers' needs individually. The Kobold system is then able to vacuum and dry-clean carpets as well as vacuum and polish hardfloors. There are also several nozzles which can be added to dust furniture, picture frames, key-boards etc. The Kobold is the only system which guarantees thorough cleaning, deep down.

The Thermomix is a unique product world-wide: it can cook, mix, steam, chop, stir, beat, pulverize, grind, juice and weigh. It is easy to use, making fresh, healthy and tasty dishes and drinks utilizing only one pot without additional equipment. So, we call it 'the smallest kitchen of the world'.

The product benefits of the Kobold and Thermonix are complex and would be difficult to communicate in conventional advertising. In our view the best way to sell such products is by in-home demonstration which is virtually impossible in a conventional retail distribution channel. We prefer to argue through the benefits of the product while retail brands compete on price and advertising.

Brand personality

The umbrella brand Vorwerk is particularly known as a direct sales company with emphasis on vacuum cleaners. The product brands, Kobold and Thermomix, are strongly related to this umbrella brand in terms of brand competence, brand benefit, brand tonality and brand imagery. Although Vorwerk sells technical household appliances, our selling approach is based on an emotional message, taking up the theme of the well-being of the family. Therefore, we have developed a message 'Our best for your family' which is the emotional product benefit for both products – in one case a cleaner home and in the other case healthier and more tasty meals. The whole spirit of family is further endorsed by the in-home demonstration of products: quite often a number of family members are there. There is no media advertising to support our brand personality although the brand features in our selling literature.

Close contact with the customer

We do not think we can overemphasize the importance of the direct selling method in underpinning our brand values. We do spend a huge amount of time, effort and money on the technical improvements of our products. Each of our products has unique features and high performance standards. However, the key advantages of direct selling are that the claims we make and the performance of the products are not advertisers' marketing puffery – they are backed by physical observation of superior product performance in the prospective purchaser's own home. The purchaser can actually use the product before buying and the sales pitch can be tailored to the individual customer's needs and concerns. For example, the product has different benefits and performance advantages on carpets and on wooden (or other hard) floors: just by observation the sales representative can see the customer's exact flooring and tailor the sales pitch accordingly.

There are some other important benefits from the selling system. Innovation is critical to our products' success and in our view, effective innovation happens through interaction with the customer and understanding his or her needs. Our eyes and ears are in our sales people who communicate with our customers. Internationally, we have over 20,000 advisers. In Germany alone, our Kobold sales force consists of more than 5,000 full-time advisers. This is equivalent to over 5,000 market researchers feeding back the customers' interests, concerns and attitudes. Thus, we are able to continually improve the quality of our products.

For the Thermomix we found that we needed to have a separate direct sales system which recognized the social aspects of food consumption. Whereas no one wants or needs to discuss their vacuum cleaning requirements in a social situation, most people love to talk about food, share their ideas and enjoy the results of a specially prepared selection of dishes. So, in some countries we introduced the Thermomix party, where the host invites a number of interested people to a party in his or her home. The product's features and functions can be easily demonstrated and the results can be tasted by everyone. In other countries, where parties are not appropriate, the products are presented in a one-to-one demonstration. Each guest is also given the opportunity to become a sales representative for Thermomix. More than 10,000 people world-wide have chosen to take up this invitation, giving them the opportunity to work part-time while bringing up a family or to use the experience as a stepping stone back into work as their family grows up.

Well-trained and motivated sales force

Our advisers are better trained and more motivated than sales people from conventional retailers. The most significant difference between retail and direct sales is that the Vorwerk advisers sell the Kobold and Thermomix actively. This means that the advisers 'create latent needs' in the consumers and do not have to wait until customers enter a store. As our people focus on a single product, they are much more familiar with the product features, the brand positioning and interactive selling techniques, and carry the positioning of the products and of Vorwerk by their demonstrations. They relay our advertising message by verbal communication which is much more powerful than printed advertising. We also invest in the continuous training of our branch managers and group leaders.

These managers are then able to train their teams accordingly. Furthermore, there are regular group meetings, in which the advisers can exchange their experiences and receive mutual support from each other.

Since our advisers are self-employed, they are highly motivated to know as much as possible about the product and to give a high quality presentation. They are entirely responsible for their own success. Additionally, we recognize their personal performance with specific tangible and intangible rewards. By comparison, retail sales people can only acquire a superficial knowledge of a number of products (which are often changing) and cannot receive the same level of training nor can they have the same motivation.

After sales activities

Our whole approach to our brand is that we do not aim to 'make a sale' but to 'create a customer' and the relationship does not finish with the purchase. In comparison to a more conventional retail environment, there is no 'middleman' as all our servicing of products is undertaken by our own people in the customer's home. We also sell consumables like filter bags, filters and cleaning powder directly to the consumer. Customer service takes place in the customer's home, supported by our call-centre which, unlike others, is not directed at making sales. Our easy-to-use system can track every customer contact and all relevant customer data.

Over time, we have implemented different customer loyalty benefits. For example, in 1996, Vorwerk founded a customer club in Germany, Club Thermomix, as a means of creating better customer dialogue. The goal of the club is not to maximize its membership but to maximize the Thermomix usage of its 60,000 members. In other words, we want to turn casual users into regular users, and regular users into avid fans. Our service is based upon encouraging the use of Thermomix through a recipe service, a telephone hotline, a customer magazine, cooking courses, special offers for household goods and gourmet tips. The club also offers services to the Thermomix representatives, who in turn use the club as a selling feature at the Thermomix parties.

In Spain, we realized that there is a real appetite for cookery classes based around the Thermomix product. In Italy, on the other hand, we found that consumers enjoy trying new recipes. Therefore, we decided to publish new Thermomix cook books annually. Every year these recipes are from a different region. The books are created by the advisers themselves. Thus, it is guaranteed that the recipes are practical, easy to follow and tasty.

Ownership and its impact on branding

Vorwerk is a family-owned company. Part of its heritage is a deeply held belief by the owners of the need to pass on the business and the brand in good health for the next generation. Like many family companies in the past, most of the brand building work was instinctive – it was something you believed in. Similarly, the relationship between the owners and their employees was based on mutual loyalty built up over the years. However, we recognized a few years ago that we needed to become more professional in the way we manage this whole process, both in terms of branding and employee relations. This was partly a result of the fact that we had grown significantly and expanded outside Germany into countries with different cultural values. Growth brings the risk of brand values being dissipated and even mis-stated. However, we also recognized that German cultural values are changing, and we cannot necessarily rely on traditional loyalties to maintain our employees' sense of belonging to the company. We therefore set about adopting a more disciplined and professional approach. We created a new corporate identity, supported by our slogan: "Our best for your family". We also codified our objectives as a company into a formal mission statement, which of necessity also included a declaration of our brand values. We believe that this has helped employees to understand our values more clearly and to recognize the part that they each play in the continued success of the company.

The results of our brand building

Vorwerk has established market leadership for its products in Germany, Austria and Italy and has achieved a good market penetration in various other European countries. This has been achieved by building market share continuously over time. We have a very specific brand image amongst consumers: high quality, durability at a premium price. This is accompanied by very high customer satisfaction and repeat purchase levels. The latter runs at over 60 per cent, which is way in excess of levels achieved by any other household appliances. Our high customer satisfaction level has a very important side benefit, as the brand is consistently recommended by word-of-mouth, both across generations in families and between friends and neighbours. Indeed, because of the durability of the products it is not unusual for older models to be passed from mother to daughter or even from grandmother to grand-daughter. In one case, a Vorwerk product was identified as a specific bequest in the grandmothers' will! Of course once the younger person has experienced the product, she will then upgrade to a newer model when circumstances allow.

Despite the absence of media advertising, we achieve high levels of awareness – usually over 60 per cent unprompted awareness in the countries in which we are represented. One reason for this is our continuous contact on a daily basis. We visit approximately 120,000 households world-wide every day, not necessarily to sell but to communicate our brand personally to individuals. As we have expanded internationally, we have followed this selling method in other countries, with careful adaptation to fit the local culture.

Direct selling in the future

We believe that direct selling will continue to grow in the future. The world-wide number of selling advisers has grown from 10 million to almost 40 million within the last 10 years and global sales are now over $100 billion through these channels. Although e-commerce will increase, it will not weaken the power of direct selling and it offers no challenge in the area of high-ticket items.

Individual customers have the potential to be extremely valuable in key sectors, which are now opening up to competition, such as telecommunications and energy. This offers the potential for direct selling, and indeed cross-selling, of products once the direct relationship is established. These products are also well-suited to the direct selling route because they require detailed understanding by the consumer who is struggling to cope with information overload. Additionally, direct selling is attractive to companies since it simplifies the value chain and enables more value to accrue to the company rather than be passed on to distributors.

Thus, we see direct selling growing in the future by continuing gains of new customers, by excluding the competing flood of information from conventional media and retailing. Direct selling also fits with broader social trends: in terms of attracting advisers, this fits well with the trend that more people want to be self-employed, work from home, and have flexible working hours. In terms of customer attitudes, it fits well with the individual's desire for tailored information, social interaction (rather than a quick pressurised sale in a store) and emotional rapport with the seller and the product. Because of the flow of information between customer and company and because of the absence of a distribution pipeline, direct selling allows much faster reaction on quality issues. The improved customer loyalty from the personal emotional relationship between customer and sales adviser increases retention and repeat purchase. In consequence, we see that direct selling will be established as an alternative distribution channel in most parts of business. But no guarantee can be given for success unless strong brand values are built through product quality, innovation and well-trained sales advisers in order to capitalize on the channel's benefits.

Conclusion

As a company our success is driven by direct access to customers, innovative products, highly motivated sales people and customer loyalty. Our brand values are integral to the delivery of such success but these values are worthless unless they are embraced by our employees and advisers. In particular, we rely on our advisers to deliver the brand values coherently as part of the sales pitch and our entire customer facing staff in their day-to-day behaviour. We don't use media advertising – we depend on our people.

Commentary

I deliberately wanted to include some unconventional even maverick brands amongst this selection of brand leaders. I believe all of us involved in brand building have to be ready to 'think out of the box' and to explore alternatives to the conventional routes which we and others have trodden before.

Vorwerk is fascinating on a number of levels: principally it demonstrates that you don't need to spend millions in media advertising to build a powerful brand. However, you do need consistency, superior products and some other means of communication.

Many traditional marketeers are patronising about direct selling but there is no reason to be so for the right product at the right time. For example, for many years it was the simplest and most effective way of collecting insurance premiums. Although it is no longer. As the chapter indicates it may prove the best way of selling utilities in the future in newly opened markets and no doubt other products too. It is not, however, a recipe for success on its own: note the importance of the superior product story, the after-sales back-up and the training for representatives which also contribute significantly to the success of Vorwerk.

11 | Wales: Can a Country Be a Brand?

ROGER PRIDE, *marketing director*

Destination marketing is fast becoming a hot subject: there can be few countries in the world which don't want to increase the number of their tourist visitors. But, as Roger Pride, marketing director of the Wales Tourist Board, explains, this simple objective is fraught with problems: a fragmented target audience with subtly different needs and providers of tourist services often have a limited vision of the brand and always have a tight purse. There are, however, lessons for other marketeers and trend custodians in how these problems are overcome.

It is probably true to say that destination marketers are not regarded as being at the cutting edge of branding philosophy and practice. Indeed many marketers contend that it is not appropriate to consider a place as a brand and that it is impossible to effectively brand a country. This is because by their very nature destinations are amorphous, delivering a wide range of products and experiences. In such an environment, contends the purist, it is impossible to control the way in which people interact with or experience the destination.

Many practitioners currently responsible for marketing destinations also regard the branding process with suspicion. Over the years the creativity of marketing departments within tourist boards has been constrained by two additional 'p's associated with destination marketing: 'politics' and 'paucity'. The politics of trying to satisfy the various factions within a destination has often led to compromise. As a result, the communication and advertising output from tourist boards has often been destination rather than consumer led, showing all aspects of the destination rather than those elements which make it special. The ubiquitous lack of substantial budgets has also led to short-term thinking which has mitigated against developing the longer term perspective necessary for building a brand.

I have always felt, however, that it is possible to use branding techniques to create a focus for differentiating holiday destinations. When I was growing up in the mining valleys of south Wales in the early sixties, children in the school playground would ask, 'Are you going on holiday this year?' There was certainly no assumption that all families actually went on holidays. Those that did almost invariably only went on one holiday a year and usually this was to the same resort year after year. In our area this meant Porthcawl and the South Wales coast. Families often stayed in the same caravan and holidayed at exactly the same time each year.

With the advent of the low-cost Mediterranean packages, the annual question in the seventies and eighties changed to 'Where are you going on holiday this year?'. The actual choice of Mediterranean destination made little difference; they were all basically the same, offering a consistent diet of sun, sand and upset stomachs. However, in choosing a holiday or short break in the 1990s, the question consumers asked themselves was 'what do we want to do on holiday this year?'. With the choice of holiday type and the range of experiences increasing, people now often decide on the holiday type before selecting the destination. Their choice of holiday type will vary with the time of year, their travelling companions and many other factors.

I believe however, that as we head into the new millennium more and more consumers will be asking, 'How do we want to feel on our holiday or short break?' As the demands of modern living become ever more stressful and the pressure on time for those in work more severe, the choice of destination and the selection of experience will assume greater importance. Consumers will want far more out of their holiday and will be choosing destinations which not only meet their core requirements but ones with which they feel an affinity. This is the territory of brands.

Tourism in Wales

Over the last one hundred years tourism has always been an important contributor to the Welsh economy. Today, it represents about 7 per cent of the Welsh GDP. It's worth more than £2 billion annually and one out of ten jobs is dependent on it. However, as a result of the factors mentioned earlier, tourism in Wales is going through structural change, competition from other destinations is intensifying and consumer needs and aspirations are ever changing.

Although it remains a substantial industry, it has the potential to grow still further. One of the factors which has inhibited growth has been Wales' image problem. This is something that we had to address. We recognized that if we were going to enhance Wales' reputation as a leisure destination, we needed a single-minded, consistent, integrated and innovative strategy. We understood however that 'branding Wales' would require a sensitive, skilled and specialist approach. When branding a country as opposed to a product or service, there is a greater variety of factors to consider – not least the way in which the process is viewed by the people living in the country and other key influencers.

Within the media and amongst traditional academics, there is still an element of suspicion and scepticism regarding the branding process. They often view the process as being superficial and cosmetic rather than seeking fundamental truths about a country. All too often the media seems to focus on the cost of the branding process – such as how much it appears to cost to create a new logo – rather than the long term benefits of brands.

Many tourism businesses in Wales also sit in the traditional and sceptical camp. One critic of the process in Wales said in a radio interview, 'Why don't they just say, "Come to bloody Wales"' – now there's a thought.

Introducing our new thinking into a public sector risk-averse culture presented a real challenge. This culture which discourages innovation is also evident amongst many key stakeholders and tourism businesses. If we kept on doing the same thing averagely well, while Wales' market share continued to decline, there might be relatively little criticism of the Wales Tourist Board. If, however, we seek to change and perhaps take a few risks along the way, our critics could have a field day. In such an environment it can become difficult to foster creativity and innovation. Some people will find one hundred reasons for not doing something rather than explore the possibilities and benefits that change would bring.

The need for a specialist and sensitive approach arises from the fundamental point that Wales the country is complex. We felt it would be wrong to believe that a single message or image could be used as a blunt instrument which has equal success with all target audiences.

Although a brand needs to be consistent, a message that will motivate a retired New York policeman to spend a week touring Wales may well be different to the message that will encourage a West Midlands factory worker to come for a weekend with his family. Ultimately however, it will be the same country, people and landscape that they experience. The trick, it seems to me, is to ensure that all messages should be based on a core set of truths about Wales which have been researched and agreed. Communications within individual market segments should draw upon these core values and communicate them in a credible, motivating and compelling way.

Through all the work we had done, it was clear that it was very difficult to isolate perceptions about Wales as a tourist destination from wider ideas of Wales the country, the nation, the political unit. Consequently, amongst potential audiences in the UK, people found it difficult to think about Wales' positive attributes as a leisure destination because they have been influenced by a cornucopia of stereotypical images from the media – of Welsh men and women and, in some cases, by the Welsh people that they may have known. It follows, therefore, that if the brand messages for Wales the tourist destination are to be fully effective, we must also address the issues relating to Wales the country.

The unique destination proposition

Our solution was to devise a brand architecture and marketing framework which was based on a tiered or layered approach with the country or domain brand giving direction and guidance. This would be supported by a tourism positioning and entry concepts tailored to the needs of individual market segments. We termed this brand communication framework the Unique Destination Proposition (UDP).

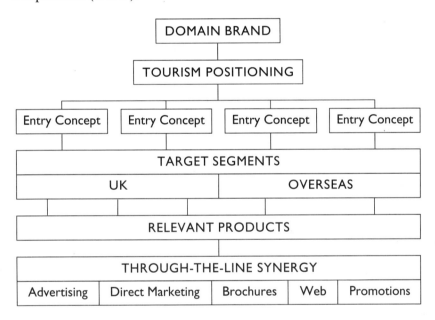

Figure 6: The key elements of the UDP framework

– **Domain brand**
An agreed branding for the country as a whole, based on the core truths or values which then guide and influence all of the country's communications needs.

– **Tourism brand**

A motivating, credible, differentiating and deliverable position for the destination.

– **Entry concepts**

A communications idea tailored to the needs to individual market segments identified through research.

– **Target segment**

Groups of potential visitors, prioritized by scoring their potential for Wales against an agreed set of criteria.

– **Relevant product**

Offering specific products from within the destination portfolio based on the needs of individual market segments, again identified through research.

– **Synergistic/integrated approach**

Ensuring that in terms of style and tone of voice, all messages and communications are mutually supportive.

The Welsh domain brand

A diverse group of public and private sector organizations in Wales decided to get together to develop a domain brand and to create a set of brand guidelines. The guidelines were used to ensure that all organizations with an interest in promoting Wales speak with the same voice. In this way, all communication would contribute to the perception of Wales as an important, lively, attractive and successful country.

A manual was created which defined the heart of the Wales domain brand and which suggested how Wales should be conveyed in pictures and in words. It also described how the core messages and values could be applied when communicating with different audiences.

The heart of this domain brand was 'In Wales you will find a passion for life – Hwyl'.

Hwyl, pronounced 'who-ill', is a Welsh word which has no direct English translation. It is a unique Welsh feeling of passion and well being.

The core message would then be supported by tangible elements – reasons to believe the core message. So a campaign to encourage inward investment in Wales would be supported by benefits such as a loyal, committed and flexible workforce and a beautiful place to live, whilst a message to attract students to Welsh universities would be supported by the benefits of a strong sense of community, the rewarding and colourful local life and high-quality education.

The manual also defined the tone of voice or personality of the brand, which is lyrical, sincere, confident, inviting, down to earth and warm.

The Wales tourism brand

The Wales Tourist Board was heavily involved in the creation of these brand guidelines and, at the same time, we set about configuring a tourism positioning for Wales which would draw upon the domain brand but which would ensure maximum resonance with potential visitors to Wales.

Considerable research was undertaken amongst our priority target audiences, both in the UK and overseas. Our original intention was to create a single tourism positioning but with separate entry concepts for the different target audiences. However, during the research it became clear that the perceptions of Wales amongst UK consumers were vastly different to those of international audiences. Moreover, we found that the consumer needs and experiences connected with domestic holidays or short breaks were very different to holidays abroad.

As was suggested earlier, in the UK market Wales' image was often neutral or negative. We did have a very loyal customer base with a high percentage of repeat visitors. However, as tastes and holiday patterns changed, many of the potential new visitors to Wales did not yet have strong enough reasons to come to Wales and many of them had negative attitudes which would take time to change. These negative views were not universal but included the perception that Wales was downmarket, lacked quality accommodation, offered little to do and had an unfriendly population. Some felt that Wales offered nothing special – yes it has mountains but Scotland's are higher, yes it has lakes but those in the Lake District are bigger, yes it has beaches but those in Cornwall and Devon are more familiar.

It was apparent, however, that often these were problems of perception rather than reality. Visitors to Wales went away with very different views. They felt that Wales was unspoiled, that there were still traditional values in Wales and a strong sense of community which translated into a safe holiday environment. They felt that the Welsh people were genuine and down to earth. They raved about how beautiful and green Wales was. They also confirmed that in comparison with similar destinations Wales was much easier to get to.

During the research process, we also tried to find out more about our target audiences and to establish what made them choose a particular destination. We also tried to get a better idea of what people wanted from a holiday or short break.

Not surprisingly we found that for many, life is stressful. Pressure to deliver at work and at home is increasing, particularly for families with working wives. This creates severe time pressures. Many within our target markets live and work in an urban environment with the resultant pressure on space – on the road, in the office and again, at home. However, although such hard-working people are often time-poor, they are usually cash-rich. So whereas every day life builds up the need for regular breaks, it is often time rather than money which is the limiting factor. As we all know, people are now getting away more often than ever but for shorter periods of time. The prime motivation for the break was the need to put something back into their lives – to relax, to recharge the batteries, to rebuild relationships and to revive their spirits.

Armed with this knowledge, we decided that the brand positioning for Wales should be 'natural revival' or 'naturally reviving'.

Wales would be 'unspoiled, down to earth, with traditional
values, genuine, green and beautiful, providing physical and spiritual revival'. And all of this hidden on England's doorstep.

In the communications brief that we developed for potential
advertising agencies to bring this positioning to life, the shorthand
for this idea was 'Wales puts back into your life what life takes out
– the antidote to every day life'.

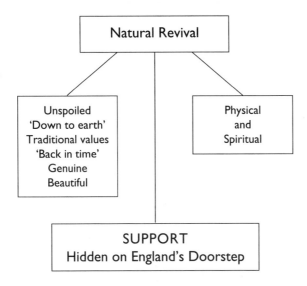

Figure 7: Wales Tourist Board UK Brand Positioning

After an exhaustive selection process we eventually chose FCA! to
bring the brand to life through a creative platform and concept
that would be effective in a wide range of potential media. We felt
that they were one of the few genuinely integrated agencies who
were media neutral. Initially they felt that the 'naturally reviving'
positioning was not differentiating enough and they undertook
additional research using their own 'Genesis' process prior to
pitching. During the process, previous visitors to Wales recalled
powerful memories and images such as dolphins and seals

swimming alongside boats in Cardigan Bay, snow falling over waterfalls in Snowdonia, walking along a north Wales beach whilst screaming at the sea on Christmas Eve and recalling simply having time for themselves as a family. On the strength of this research FCA! confirmed natural revival as being the appropriate brand positioning.

The campaign that resulted developed specific creative applications for each target segment. All of these were linked by a very distinctive creative style and supported by the strapline – 'Wales two hours and a million miles away'. The poster, television and direct marketing execution showed black and white images of people within the target markets in stressful everyday situations and contrasted these with evocative, colourful images of the same people being 'revived' in Wales. We also developed a number of innovative ideas such as dirty grimy vans driving through London and Birmingham with the line 'Clean Air Is Two Hours Away' finger-written on the back of the vans. We also distributed air fresheners to London taxi drivers with the line 'Real Fresh Air Is Only Two Hours Away'.

The campaign achieved significant stand-out from other destination campaigns and, despite very challenging marketing conditions for domestic holidays, achieved encouraging results. Wales' share of trips and spend increased. Brochure enquiries rose from 140,000 in 1998 to 240,000 in 1999. Monitoring research revealed increases in awareness and ranking. Finally, to date, the campaign has won fifteen national and international awards including ones from the Chartered Institute of Marketing and Travel Industry Groups and Multi Media Campaign of the Year Award in 1998, beating off competition from such recognized brands as Virgin Atlantic, British Airways and Thomson Holidays.

The international positioning

Potential overseas visitors to Wales did not have the same negative perceptions of Wales as many of their UK counterparts. Overseas visitors were, in general, much more interested in messages about Wales which emphasized Wales distinctiveness. The Welsh language, Celtic heritage and the Welsh people were all found to be motivating factors to target segments which would have relatively little appeal to our core English markets.

We also discovered that often the needs which have been satisfied from a main overseas holiday were very different to those satisfied on a domestic short break. For domestic holidays intrinsic benefits such as relaxation, recharging the batteries and rest predominate. People want more from holidays overseas. These can be classified as extrinsic benefits such as adventure, excitement and enrichment.

We decided therefore that the potentially more powerful positioning of 'inspiring recreation' was appropriate for (and acceptable to) our target markets overseas. We tested various entry concepts to this overseas positioning and eventually selected the 'land of nature and legend' platform for all consumer communication and the 'inspiring ideas' concept for business tourism communication.

Brand guidelines for the 'land of nature and legend' idea were developed in conjunction with the British Tourist Authority, who deliver much of the international communication about Wales. The following extract from these guidelines demonstrates that whilst the positioning is specific to the needs of overseas markets, it is compatible and complementary to the UK positioning.

- Wales is honest, welcoming and romantic. It is a country to inspire and revive.
- Wales holds a passion which is drawn from a heritage of poetry and song, legend and mystery. There is a spirituality about the natural and dramatic beauty of the countryside. Wales is a land of nature and legend.
- Wales is atmospheric and mystical but down to earth and strong. Its countryside has a compelling beauty.
- There is nothing trivial about the romanticism of Wales; ancient tombs lend an air of mystery while the great Welsh castles appear part of the solid natural Welsh landscape. Both are rich in the country's legend and myth.

- There is lyricism in the people. The Welsh language is at the heart of the country's poetic tradition. The poetry of Wales may be lyrical but is never simply decorative. It springs from the straightforwardness, warmth and openness of the Welsh people. It is real poetry rung from the reality of everyday lives.

The future

There is little doubt that Wales has made considerable progress in the development of an effective brand communications framework. Within the Wales Tourist Board we feel we have played a key role in this process. It is clear, however, that we are still at the start of the process. Wales still does not enjoy the financial and economic benefits that should accompany a strong brand. We have not yet fully developed the identity premium. The core values and truths identified need to form the basis of a framework which allows communication in a wide variety of circumstances and across many industry sectors. This needs to be an inclusive process and the work carried out to date provides a good starting point. We need to draw upon the tangible attributes such as our dramatic uplifting landscape, our strong sense of community, our high-quality education, our loyal and committed workforce, our success in music and the arts and our passion for sports in order to create strong emotional linkages.

The successful branding of Wales will not happen automatically but it is vital that the strategy is rooted in reality and is built upon the belief of the people living and working in Wales. The process needs to be carefully managed and communicated. Crucial to its success in the future will be a commitment and leadership from the highest government levels in Wales. This has already been demonstrated with the new first minister for Wales, Rhodri Morgan, forming a new branding group. The Welsh Assembly has realized that we are currently presented with the unique opportunity to achieve Wales' potential on a world stage.

Within the Wales Tourist Board we will now review and evolve our tourism positioning. We want to ensure that the people representing the Wales Tourist Board (and therefore Wales) fully represent and convey the personality of the country. We recognize that we need to give clearer guidance to our stakeholders within the tourism industry in Wales so that they too can fully support the brand positioning and the brand process. The unique destination proposition that we have created will be the template on which we build our future branding strategy.

Commentary

I have to declare an interest in Wales since Springpoint was responsible for the brand positioning and the brand book of Wales. I hope I can produce an objective view.

The historical marketing of destinations in the UK was for the shrinking market of the long summer holiday, which had experienced intense competition from low-cost/reliably hot weather destinations in Europe. The new opportunity came from short breaks – whether taken by dual-income families, affluent singles or the 'grey/wrinklies', either retired or after dependent children had left home. This market wanted something different which Wales is uniquely able to provide because of its geographic convenience.

Even having understood this change, it is patently obvious that the target audience is diverse and it will be hard to be all things to all men. Again it is important to try to identify broad truths which appeal to all for mass marketing which can be supported by more targeted offers to the specific target audience.

At the same time it is possible to have a slightly different positioning in overseas markets since overlap of reading/viewing/listening will be minimal.

The influence of politics is important, since politicians generally have little grasp of branding, through an instinctive sense of the economic importance of tourism. It is interesting in this case that the impetus for branding was not just tourism but also inward investment and higher education. This helped the notion of the domain brand so all promotion of the country was focused on a single theme.

12 | Wal-Mart Asda: The Revival of a Brand

ALLAN LEIGHTON, *former CEO Asda and*
RICHARD BAKER, *group marketing director Asda*
Wal-Mart

This is a story about two retailer brands. The first is Asda, which was founded over thirty years ago in the north of England, and the second Wal-Mart, which began when Sam Walton opened his first Wal-Mart store in the southern US state of Arkansas in 1962. And how, despite being continents apart, over the years these two brands developed with such a similar set of values and visions that the acquisition of Asda in 1999 by Wal-Mart for £6.7 billion (although at the time the biggest cash transaction between companies in the two countries) was successfully carried out in the short space of just six days. Allan Leighton, former chief executive of Asda and Richard Baker, group marketing director of Asda Wal-Mart, explain the company's strategy.

The revival of a brand

In 1999 Asda had sales of £8.8 billion and profits of £317 million. But what could be called the first defining moment in its history stretches back a quarter of a century to when, a few years into its existence, the company decided to do some advertising. Wary of dealing with the big London advertising agencies, the founders hired some people who made an important discovery. Asda shoppers would reject products if they perceived that the price was not 'Asda' price – if, in other words, it was too high. So that became the theme of the advertising: shoppers at Asda could save 10–15 per cent of the annual grocery bill in any one home. The pocket-tapping came in at the same time.

By the time I arrived in early 1992 as group marketing director those values had eroded. But research showed that even though some of these ideas hadn't been used in five years, the biggest recall was that of the 'Asda price' and the pocket tapping. So what you could call the next defining moment came eight to nine years ago when I decided we should revisit that approach and so with our agency, Publicis, we used the concept for new ads.

Asda's story, however, is about far more than just reviving the advertising. Coming to Asda from the confectionery group Mars, I was shocked to find that the company saw itself as a retailer first, and seemed to put customers last. That's the opposite at a branded business like Mars, where the customers always came first. Also, at Mars everyone would just pop into each other's offices – it didn't matter who you were. This wasn't the case at Asda. This was the only environment that I knew worked, so we had to change it. There are, after all, only two things that are important in a business. One is the way you look after your people and the other is the way you look after customers. If you don't look after your people they won't look after your customers.

The Asda culture has now changed significantly. Everybody is on first name terms, there are open-plan offices, no car parking spaces, and no directors' dining room. It didn't have anything to do with the local Yorkshire culture, although that probably made it easier. It still took us three years for people to subscribe to this change in culture, because lots of people like having car parking spaces, big offices, different carpets. Our approach isn't everyone's cup of tea.

Bear in mind, though, this more informal culture is also driven for real commercial reasons like speed of communications and having an ear to the ground, which are fundamental in running businesses. And the bigger the business, the more fundamental they are. Unfortunately, the bigger the business is, usually the further people are away from this. So the reason to do it was not just because it seemed a nice thing to do but because there was a lot of commercial logic to it. I would call it one of Asda's critical success factors.

Creating the brand context

Our philosophy is that all organizations need to have some context, and that the context is generally set by three things. One is a mission statement, the second is the company's purpose and the third is its values. And if you have got businesses that don't have these three things, then they don't work because there's no context for the people in the organization. And with 100,000 employees it's very important they fully understand the context of the business.

Take the mission statement first. When it comes to mission statements, I've always said the best way to describe them is to ask what do you want to be when you grow up. And if you can't say what you want to be when you grow up you'll never grow up. Also, the great thing about mission statements is you never quite get there. You need to have something you can aim at. So our mission is straightforward: we aim to be Britain's best-value fresh food and clothing superstore.

That's pretty important because, first, we are British and, second, if you are not in fresh food you are not in the business. When we began this journey we were very bad at it – and we are now pretty good at it because we have focused on it as part of what we are trying to do. Clothing is there because with the George range we have something that is hard to copy and so it has become a big part of the competitive difference. And we say superstores because we don't have small stores, and best value because that's what we have to be and what we are.

So that's our mission. Purpose is always dead straightforward: it has to begin with 'satisfied' because that's the name of the game. You either satisfy customers or you don't. So our purpose is satisfying the weekly shopping needs of ordinary working people and their families. Weekly because we are a superstore. Ordinary working people because they are the middle market in Britain. All our range, from clothing through to general merchandise, means that we can, more than anyone else, satisfy family shopping under one roof. Our customers work hard, they are not overpaid, they are very conscious of how they spend their money and they want value – it's not an option to give it to them or not.

And we also have a number of values. We are all colleagues – one team – because that's what we are. And those values, every one of them, include the word we. That says it doesn't matter who you are in this organization, you are the same. And that includes being part of the selling machine because it's through selling that we make our service legendary. We are not buyers, or retailers – we are here to sell things, and we sell things because they are outstanding value, whether you are in human resources, or logistics, or you work on the check-out.

We also hate waste. This isn't what you throw in the bin but waste of time, money, energy and effort, and that's crucial because it makes you much more low cost, more conscious, more productive and basically faster. Speed and turnaround time is a piece of competitive edge we've been able to create and which I think is on the frontier of how companies operate. Businesses like ours are made up of lots of little changes, so it is everybody's responsibility in some way every day to improve the business.

Brand integrity starts on the shop floor

You could say that CEO in my case doesn't stand for chief executive officer but for context executive officer because you can't have any culture if you haven't got any context. And everybody thinks you can stick culture into a syringe and bang it in peoples' arms. It doesn't work like that. The context is what do we do, what we stand for, what are we here to achieve. It's said that the CEO is, in many ways, the custodian of the brand. I have a different slant on it. It's true that I'm very protective of the brand and get upset when things get changed and if people do things that don't underpin it. But I think our only chance is to have 100,000 people who understand what it is we are trying to do, because they won't let the integrity of the brand down.

To further that we try and recruit friendly colleagues who are motivated to sell because service comes from the heart, not from manuals. If you don't recruit the right people, those who are genuinely and generally positive, who are capable of smiling and have a really good sense of humour and want to be part of a team, then it doesn't matter how you train them. People who don't like being nice to people can't be trained to be nice. That's where it all comes from. So you have to recruit friendly people who like to sell.

That's why our recruitment is different from everyone else's. We don't have individual recruitment but group selection. We get twenty people in for a couple of hours and give them a crazy task to do, like design a new packet of cornflakes as a group. And then we'll get them to wander around the shop floor so we can watch them meet customers and colleagues. Do they smile and talk to them? Because we can train anyone to do the job but you can't train everyone to like people.

Every four weeks or so we survey around 20,000 colleagues to see how they feel about the business. The number one question is – do you enjoy working in this store? When I see that 94 per cent of colleagues overall say they enjoy working in their stores I don't have to read further because I know that if people enjoy what they are doing then every other axis beneath that will be positive.

To me, the stores are the heroes in this business. Every twelve weeks for the last eight years I have visited every store manager. This can take up a total of three and a half days of my time, but that doesn't matter because they are very important to us. On average they each have £50 million sales and 500 colleagues so being close to them and listening to what they say are crucial. They are also the most powerful lobby – which is exactly what they should be – for improvements in our operations, where we could do things better, and how we manage our people.

The store managers are very autonomous but they have freedom within a framework. 75–80 per cent of what they do is prescribed across the company – such as the corporate identity – but 20 per cent is locally flexible. This 20 per cent which is locally flexible is often what makes a difference between stores. So active selling, sampling, relationships with community and charities, are all areas that are decided and executed locally.

So I am the last person who can do anything about our brand consistency. And the marketing director is the second last, and the ad agency the third last. Most of us don't understand this.

Exploiting the brand potential

In any company or brand you have to try and differentiate as much as you can and find the ingredients, whether they be products you eat or drive or shop in, that are hard to copy and unmatchable. It's a combination of the uniqueness and unmatchability of products that creates great brands – which is why there aren't very many of them because this combination is hard to achieve.

Take what we've done with the George brand. The idea of George is very straightforward. It's basically high street clothing at Asda prices. So the Asda connection is very strong in the pricing. But it's always branded as George, and George is seen to be very much part of the underpinning of Asda. We exploded the myth that you couldn't buy decent clothing in supermarkets and will continue to develop the George brand with the aim of making it the biggest clothing brand in Europe within the next five years.

And we'll continue to extend the Asda brand into areas where we feel we can deliver better value than anyone else. The problem with brand extensions is that most of them dilute the core brand values and are done because the sales of the core brand are slowing down. Which, if you think about it, is completely the wrong thing to do. You need to focus on why the core brand is slowing down. Surfing off the back of brands generally kills them in the end. But if you have a great core proposition, then you should only extend it if it absolutely fits and enhances the image.

For example, our own-label products are a huge extension of the Asda brand. They now account for 40 per cent of grocery. We have also created Asda Fresh which is fresh food of delicatessen and high street type quality at Asda prices. Asda @ Home is our home delivery business, based on the Internet, fax, and telephone and run from two warehouse centres in London – in Croydon and Watford. Because we have very low penetration in London, I call them stealth stores because they are in areas where we don't have many stores. So for us these largely generate net incremental sales whereas for other retailers there is the danger of home shopping cannibalizing sales. We've also moved into the fixed-line telephone market with Asda Calltime, which offers residential customers the lowest prices you can get. So overall the idea is to extend it to where what you can offer is consistent with the brand.

Welcome to Wal-Mart

Even more significantly, the Asda brand is now part of Wal-Mart. What makes this so amazing is that Wal-Mart and Asda values are exactly the same. I've known the Wal-Mart team for five years and been a fan much longer than that. This has obviously helped tremendously. And it's not surprising because the Asda business philosophy has primarily been based on two companies. One is Wal-Mart and the other is Mars. My Mars experience taught me about the way in which the people should be managed. From Wal-Mart we learned not just about how to treat people with integrity but also about trading and the positioning of value.

I always thought it would be good in terms of alignment and I use that word purposefully because what tends to happen to most mergers and acquisitions is that when one company buys or merges with another the culture of the dominant company gets imposed on the other. People call it integration and what they mean is we're just going to tell everybody what to do. Because we have been very conscious of this we have set up business alignment teams with the best people in each one of the divisions working on aligning all parts of the business.

When you embark on a marriage like this, the courtship and then the engagement are all exciting, with the day of the announcement probably the high point. But then the real work starts. In the first phase you have to see how it all works, how the bits and pieces fit together. And you get through the getting-along phase, where everybody is testing each other out before you finally can get down to working together. And we have got from the first to second phase remarkably quickly because what we are trying to do between the businesses is for Asda to create a better Wal-Mart, not a worse Wal-Mart, and for Wal-Mart to create a better Asda, not a worse Asda.

For example, the Asda store managers have been talking to each other all the time. And we've expanded that now since we became part of Wal-Mart. Our guys have been over there teaching the US store managers about food and the US food managers have been over here teaching our guys about general merchandise. And each manager here has a buddy store in the US. So each one of the Asda store managers has been to the US and worked in the super-centre buddy store for a week and the US managers are now coming over here to work in our stores here for a week. They talk to each other once a week and exchange ideas. That's how you really get a team to work.

Wal-Mart CEO Lee Scott and I have been managing this at the top of the organization in order to get that piece of thinking into the business. And so here we are a year on better aligned than any acquisition or merger of this scale before. We now have a higher score for enjoyment among colleagues than a year ago, and a higher 'feeling secure' score. Our share-save scheme had the highest take-up of any share-save scheme in the history of any British business. So the colleague base is absolutely bedded into this.

What's important is that employees feel ownership: about 75 per cent of the Asda population of 100,000 own all our shares, which means that 75,000 staff members own shares, while 54,000 have the share-save option. We have also developed an all-colleague bonus programme which means that every single person in the company earns a bonus on the performance of their brand locally. So if the Southgate store delivers its profitability because it delivers its brand, then everyone in the store gets a bonus. The company doesn't have to hit it. It's the store. That's my point – if you can get this absolutely localized, where the context is understood locally, the execution is done locally and everybody shares in the performance, you have almost got to utopia in terms of what I call the brand tentacles.

Getting the best from brands

The Asda brand is very powerful in the UK. It stands for value. And the Wal-Mart brand is very powerful globally and stands for value. It is not understating it to call Wal-Mart a phenomenon. Is it any surprise that since we were bought by Wal-Mart, prices in every single UK retail business have come down by 2 per cent? Although everybody tries to pretend they were going to do it anyway, you can almost point to the very day they did this. That's the first thing. The second is that the 10 per cent of the population that didn't shop at Asda prior to this now shop at Asda with the same store base. They decide to have a look at us because of Wal-Mart. I've never seen anything like this.

And thirdly I doubt if there has been a single newspaper in the last year that every day or every second day at most doesn't mention the name Wal-Mart, so the brand recognition of Wal-Mart in the UK is reaching above 80 per cent. So what we will do on the branding front is combine the best of both worlds. We will build supercentres which will be called Asda Wal-Mart while all the stores which are the non-supercentres will be branded Asda. With these supercentres you have two great value brands side by side. You have Asda, which is powerful in its own right, backed up by being a member of the Wal-Mart family.

Managing across borders

When I say 'we' I mean Wal-Mart because I am no longer responsible for the day-to-day management at Asda but for Wal-Mart in

Europe as a whole. My job has two to three parts. Number one is to continue to provide the context – and the relevant context – for whatever market we are in. The second is to be a teacher. I'm there to help people learn from what I know. The third thing is to make sure we recruit excellent people, because that's fundamental. All this effort lives and dies without good people. John Mars always said brands don't die – people kill brands. Marks & Spencer, for example, was badly managed. The brand didn't decide it wasn't going to do well one day. If you want great brands get great people.

There are several approaches to managing in different cultures. One is never have a management team that has no local people from the country. The country nationals should always be the majority because they understand it. But I also quite like the idea that 30 per cent of the top management population is international. And in Germany we have Germans, Italians, Spaniards, Canadians, some Americans and British, so it's a nice mix. Probably about 50 per cent of the top management is German. What I'd like to get to is having the 50 per cent who are international able to speak the language.

A lot is made of the problems in translating 'American-ness' to other countries but I think it's a myth that the 'have a nice day' approach to service doesn't travel. Asda, for example, has had greeters for six years. They are the most popular people we have, with most of them over the age of fifty. Someone told me years ago that if you walk down the street and smile at someone they will smile back. So why not do it? There isn't anyone I've ever seen in any of our stores who has been offended by the greeters. Everyone has looked at what we at Asda have done and been cynical, but we have grown and thrived. Everyone criticizes Wal-Mart's approach but in twenty-five years it has come from nothing to be one of the biggest companies in the world.

Just think. Together we have a million associates. And there are only two other enterprises that have more than a million people. One is the Russian army. And the other one is the Indian National Railway, with three and a half million people. It is impossible to be so wrong as everybody thinks we are about everything and still to have grown so much. The millions of customers who shop with us are not all shopping with us because they don't like the greeters or chanting.

Taking the brand online

Wal-Mart has been slow in deciding its online proposition. But now that we have, we are not wasting any time. And we have a lot going for us because in my view our Internet business is about three things. First is about creating the brand, and we probably have the best brand in the world to represent value. The reason I believe businesses like boo.com ran into problems is that they had to spend a great deal of money establishing something. So you have to have a strong brand which is global in its translation because the Internet by its definition is a global business.

The second thing is you have to have very good procurement. You have to buy at very low prices. That's what we should be able to do more than anyone else. Thirdly, you have to have the best fulfilment in the world. And if big retailers can do anything well, they can do procurement and fulfilment. I think it's right for Wal-Mart.com to concentrate on merchandise because it is high-ticket price and high margin and the economics are very different from food, which has fulfilment problems of its own. Everyone there is still trying to find the right model.

As all the Internet noise and hype dies down, there will be many more boo.coms. The strong brick brands will become the strong click brands. Wal-Mart will continue to grow and out-perform and move into new markets, look at new formats, and develop e-commerce.

Biggest is not always best

In my view there are river companies and puddle companies. The river companies stand the test of time, like rivers. They've been around a long time and sometimes they flow fast, and sometimes slowly, and sometimes they burst their banks and if there is an obstacle in the way they tend to find their own natural way around the obstacle. That's what great companies are like. Puddle companies are fine till the sun comes out and then they dry up. You have to decide whether you are a river or puddle company.

River companies have always had a very strong sense of context, a strong mission, purpose and values, because chief executives come and go. That's why you have to have this imbued in the organization so if anyone at the top of the company tries to change that the rest of the organization would revolt. That's what you want.

The other thing is that everyone thinks that river companies have to be big companies. It's not that, nor is it about the big eating the small. It's about the fast eating the slow. You are much better to be fast than big. To say the only way you can be world class is to be global is wrong. It doesn't matter if you are a one-shop or one-factory or one-brand business and you are national–local rather than global. You still have to be world class. People don't differentiate between being world class and world active – but they are completely different. A lot of the companies and brands that are world active are not world class.

I always look at whoever is the best at whatever they are doing. There is a great company in the US called Gabberts Furniture with twelve stores in Minnesota. They are world class, not world active. This company knocks your socks off – it's a great business to watch. And probably 10 per cent of what we have been doing at Asda over the last few years came from Herb Kelleher at Southwest Airlines, who is fantastic at motivating his staff, which works through to great service. So I read about these companies, talk to people, and make sure we benchmark ourselves against who's the best and who's doing well, whether they have one or 1,000 shops.

Wal-Mart just happens to add up to be the biggest retailer in the world. It started with one shop and in that shop Sam Walton tried to be world class. He tried to be the best and eventually ended up being the biggest. And that's the way you have to do things. If you aren't the best you won't be the biggest. Or, if you are, you won't be for very long.

Addendum

Allan Leighton recently appointed Richard Baker as group marketing director of Asda. Richard was invited to comment on how the story of these two retailers brands has progressed since Allan wrote this chapter.

Wal-Mart have proved to be perfect foster parents. We have successfully married two brands together and we are now genuinely delivering the best of both. We have retained the identity of the Asda brand and we have not turned Asda into a Wal-Mart. Instead, we have a better Asda. As Lee Scott, president and chief executive, Wal-Mart said, 'We will not tell you to do anything, but we'll invite you to come and delve into the toybox and see what you like most.'

Asda continues to be led by a local team. Today, Asda is setting new records in customer loyalty, colleague loyalty share and profits. In the *Sunday Times* top 500 'best company to work in' league table, Asda came fifth and the four companies above Asda were all private companies. This is a remarkable success story and is one of the exceptions in the history of mergers and acquisitions.

Commentary

The regeneration of the Asda brand is an outstanding success story and, was of course, featured in *Brand Warriors*. This study shows that this renaissance has continued under the stewardship of Allan Leighton. He shows all the spirit of a true brand warrior in the depth of his involvement in the brand and in the recognition that head office does not have a monopoly of wisdom. The effort to tap into the contribution of every store manager is, in my view, truly awe-inspiring and helps explain their success.

You might have thought that Wal-Mart, arguably the world's most successful mass retailer, would feel that it had little to learn from its UK acquisition. But no, we see that there are specifics where Wal-Mart quickly acknowledged that there were transferable skills from the UK to the US (as well as the other way round). How refreshing.

Finally, we often hear talk about how this idea or service initiative won't travel because it is rooted in local culture. Again Asda shows us that with a more open-minded approach, the key task becomes adaptation not slavish adoption. This process of adapting the best in the world to suit local needs is surely the way forward for all global businesses.

13 | Yahoo!: The Beginnings of a Brand

JERRY YANG, *co-founder and chief Yahoo!*
KAREN EDWARDS *senior vice president*

Is is hard to believe that in the space of just six years Yahoo! has moved from a garage in Stanford to being the most visited site on the World Wide Web, with over 185 million users over six years. Of course the heady growth of Internet usage accounts for part of this growth. But Yahoo! has not been short of competitors throughout this time so its achievements in both business growth and in brand creation have been formidable.

The beginnings of a brand

Yahoo! is a young brand in both senses of the word: not only is it only a few years old, but it focuses its appeal on the young at heart. Its founders, Jerry Yang and David Filo, were two post graduate students at Stanford University who began to explore the Internet as a diversion from their doctoral theses. They decided to create a list of all the interesting sites which they were discovering on the Net, thus creating a directory, which was effectively a road map to finding useful, interesting or entertaining content on the Internet. This site was called 'David and Jerry's Guide to the World Wide Web'.

While we are now accustomed to everyone from grandmothers to primary school pupils accessing the Internet, at the time the usage was largely confined to academic, military and government – a closely linked group of people with very specific needs. For the individual consumer the Internet was a chaotic mystery – inherently fascinating but daunting to try to find what you want. More and more users, encouraged by word-of-mouth, came to the site and Jerry and David's hobby began to take on a life of its own. Eventually the duo decided that they needed a new name for their pet project. At the time, a lot of Internet sites began with the letters 'ya' so Jerry and David looked in the dictionary for a suitable name. They found 'Yahoo' and felt it described their lifestyle as postgraduate students very well. So they added an exclamation mark and a brand was born.

The name immediately defined a distinct personality and a sense of fun that was possible on the Internet. The early users were very much pioneers: those who knew and used Yahoo! were given the sense of belonging to a club. We encouraged this interaction with the brand, and this sense of discovery, through the use of the slightly provocative, call to action – 'Do you Yahoo!?'

In these early days brand promotion was limited to word-of-mouth recommendation, which is nearly always vital for mould-breaking brands to fuel their growth. At last users could find a place where people like them had transformed chaos into a useful guide to the Internet. This feeling of involvement, from a very early stage, was the basis for a close relationship between Yahoo! and its users, which is very much alive today. Yahoo! users identify with our brand values and brand personality and there is still very much a sense of discovery associated with the Yahoo! experience.

> The Yahoo! brand has always been differentiated from its competitors because of its focus on consumers. The brand focuses on bringing a sense of ease, fun, and relevance to users worldwide. First, there is the brand name itself, Yahoo! which is distinctive, memorable and evocative. It allowed the company to transcend language and other global barriers and enabled it to evolve into diverse areas of business without limiting definition. Second, beyond product efficacy, the brand is about an emotional attachment, creating a sense of a trusted friend to its users and clients. Yahoo! enabled and empowered people. The ability to achieve this successfully has contributed greatly towards growing

Yahoo! to be a full-service network and from there to the number one Internet brand world-wide.

Jerry Yang, co-founder and chief Yahoo!

Core values

At the heart of every great brand there are some clear core values and a distinctive brand personality – Yahoo! is no different.

Yahoo! as a word is fun and friendly – in fact, people smile even when mentioning it. Fun and friendly thus forms the heart of the Yahoo! brand and is present in all consumer communications. (Examples include the human magic moments played out in Yahoo!'s TV advertising; buzz marketing such as Internet-enabled Moo Cows and the New York Parade; setting up Yahoo! shops on the high street to provide stressed shoppers with a chill-out zone where they can shop online.)

However, we knew that just being fun and friendly was, in itself, not a strong or distinctive enough proposition. It did not reflect the credibility of the product, built on a secure technological plat-form but very much designed by human beings, with other people in mind.

Thus, Yahoo! is more fun and friendly, it is also human, trustworthy, reliable, and easy to use. Yahoo! was at the time a hierarchical structure of websites built by human editors. At the beginning, Yahoo! was a directory, built by human beings, provid-ing users with easy, comprehensive and intuitive access to the best of the Web. So it was entirely true and evident to the user that Yahoo! was a very human brand. Equally, it has been a fundamental criterion of our technological platform and our design that Yahoo! is easy to use. Again we didn't need to trumpet our technology – the users experience showed how simple it was (and remains).

By contrast trust and reliability have to be earned – you can't say to consumers 'trust me' when you are a new brand. However it is remarkable that the close relationship between consumers and the brand have allowed these values to develop very quickly so that Yahoo! has become the brand that users trust not only with their personal information but also their financial information. Clearly this would not be possible with just a fun and friendly brand.

These brand values also reflect the quality of the product that is delivered. Our product managers endeavour to avoid gimmicks and unnecessary design that could slow download speeds and frustrate the end user. Equally Yahoo! is very careful to control the amount and type of advertising each user is exposed to. Even with a brand that people feel close to, we know that our competitors are always just 'one click away'.

Developing new services

We knew right from the beginning that if Yahoo! were to become an essential part of people's lives, it would have to develop beyond just the initial directory. We aspired to develop a brand that users returned to day after day and spent more and more time at each time they visited. Our guiding philosophy was, and is, to provide users with the only place they needed to go to find anything, connect with anyone and buy or sell anything.

As a result we embarked on a programme of service enhancements, which fundamentally changed the way people saw and used Yahoo!

One of the early additions was Yahoo! mail and this really did change the way people saw us. Once a consumer has a Yahoo! e-mail account it becomes part of their daily life. It is no longer a departure site on the Internet, which one dips in and out of as needs dictate, but an essential part of our daily routine. In fact, it is now in many countries the site where people spend the most time every month. And the more time is spent, the more affinity is felt with the brand.

We took this a stage further with the creation of My Yahoo!, which enables consumers to personalize his or her Yahoo! experience by choosing which information they want to be displayed. For example, you can set up your own stock portfolio, choose to display your horoscope, news from the sports teams you support, etc.

We also recognized that the Web was fast becoming an integral way in which individuals and organizations conducted their daily lives. We noticed how community organizations and interest groups wanted to have easy access to providing local citizens or members with information and to have simple information exchange. Yahoo! community sites were developed to enable this. At the same time, we also strengthened the relationship between Yahoo! and its customers in two ways: we were doing something they really wanted and we were popping up unexpectedly as they browsed for information, thus maintaining awareness.

Shopping on the Internet

All of us at Yahoo! believe that the Internet has created a paradigm shift in consumer behaviour. For many it has become the preferred way to communicate with their friends, look for information, meet new friends, arrange holidays and, increasingly, to go shopping.

We therefore saw the creation of Yahoo! shopping as critical to our continued growth. In designing our shopping offer, we wanted to build on our core competencies of content aggregation and of helping people connect as we recognized that we lacked the classic retail competencies of stock management and logistics. We chose to be a shopping mall rather than a retailer. Just as our clubs and chat rooms enable people to connect, Yahoo! shopping enables retailers and customers to connect with each other.

This also enhances the user experience, since we enable the shopper to have maximum choice in any category. In addition to the mass-market retailers who inevitably want to be there, we also provide access to specialist retailers who might not be available locally. In addition, the shopper can compare prices, product features and product availability across a variety of merchants just as he or she might do in a shopping mall but with greater choice and in less time.

Developing internationally

Given the global nature of the Internet, it was clear right from early on that Yahoo! had to be global and in 1996 we made the decision to expand internationally. Now over 40 per cent of our revenues come from outside the US.

We recognized that we could not expect users around the world to be satisfied with yahoo.com, an English language site with an American focus. On the other hand we wanted to create consistency in our global brand since we could not allow our brand values or personality to be different around the world. We created local-language Yahoo! sites – maintaining our global values, simple and easy-to-use design, but harnessing the knowledge of local managers. Our local sites provide local content, local communities and a true local identity.

We are careful to maintain a global look and feel by using a company-wide template for our websites, designed to build the brand and leverage its underlying technology on a global scale. The Yahoo! logo (with the relevant country's name beneath it) sits top and centre on every site. The buttons that link to Yahoo's stickiest applications – Yahoo! mail, Yahoo! Messenger, My Yahoo, and Yahoo! auctions – are positioned alongside. The shopping box comes next, followed by the directories, each one with 14 categories. Sponsors are always listed on the right. Company information, including links to other Yahoo! sites, is listed at the bottom. In other words, language apart, a Yahoo site is instantly recognizable wherever in the world it originates. And the fundamental benefits of 'find', 'connect' and 'purchase' are the same the world over.

So we have established our overseas operations, for the most part, by setting up local subsidiary companies predominantly staffed by local nationals. However each local site does not have a totally free rein: our core competence is ease-of-use and the simplicity of our site and there can be no deviation from this. Other services and content are locally decided. For example, we have created an education area on the Japanese site reflecting the importance and value put on education by the Japanese people. The Hong Kong site has a depth of financial information that reflects the level of local financial interest and focus on the stock market and the Brazil site focuses its depth of offering on entertainment and music to reflect its local values. We are now established in twenty-four countries in twelve languages, with more than thirty offices world-wide.

However, the greatest challenge is maintaining the brand values while we continue to adapt locally. This means recognizing that fun may be differently interpreted in Singapore than it is in Spain. We are lucky, however, that Yahoo! elicits good vibes (Yahoo! vibes) in every language – or at least every language so far!

In most local markets, we face both global and local competitors, and therefore strive to provide the very best of the Net locally with the global richness to enable users to expand their horizons. In addition, our brand differentiation is key to our success – our commitment to remain true to our brand values and be the human face of the Internet is vital in sustaining our competitive differentiation.

Our commitment to localization in terms of products, services and marketing communication, backed by international resources, is a strong factor in our success outside North America. We realized early on that to be true to our values we could not act as an American company abroad but had to invest in international infrastructure and people.

Managing growth

One of our major challenges has been managing our brand values while growing at a heady pace. For example, just in terms of employees we have grown from seventeen when I joined to over 3,000 now. The key issue is how to keep them all on the same page.

For us the brand is the beacon, which keeps everyone focused on the same objectives. All our new recruits are quickly trained in the key values and attributes of the brand, which are simple and easy to understand. Once they are assimilated, it becomes a self-fulfilling prophecy because all our people want to work with this brand. Perhaps it is also important to note that our senior management, including the founders, are there because they want to be there and they are committed to the brand and its brand values. This permeates quickly through the organization.

We also went through the experience of becoming a public company (with an IPO) when we were relatively young – we only had one hundred employees. We have actually found this helpful. It maintains a focus on our financial performance and in our case enabled us to ensure our people and our investors understand the importance of long-term brand building. It also helped develop the trustworthy/reliable dimensions of our values since the public offering demonstrated that we were a company there for tomorrow, not just here today. We have tried to reinforce this by providing investor/press information which is timely, simple and where appropriate supported by third party information which demonstrates management commitment to communication.

Building a brand in cyberspace

An Internet brand is unusual. There is nothing physical to touch except some pieces of paper if you want them. It is a service, but unlike a bank or airline, we have no direct contact with the people delivering the service yet the brand still plays a very important part in people's lives. We therefore place huge emphasis on continuous improvements to functionality and maintaining our core values of speed and ease of use. Of course in the early days of the brand in each country we needed to build awareness and to stimulate trial. Now, in many markets, we have gone beyond just building brand awareness and are more about building an emotional connection with our users. Again the creation of an Internet brand is unusual: advertising and other promotional activity outside the site can be very important, much of our brand relationship with our customers is about their experience with the product – what happens when each one switches on their computer in the morning.

A mistake that some of the start-up dot-com companies are making is investing significant spend in creating awareness quickly but with no substance behind it. There is no emotional connection that the individual consumer can make and no integrated approach to marketing. It seems like they are just wanting to make some noise by getting out there with advertising but then they discovering that consumers have an awareness but little understanding of the proposition and even less empathy with the brand.

So our approach has been very much integrated: we use advertising, promotions, direct marketing and other communication vehicles on the site, alongside advertising in other media, public relations, co-marketing with like-minded brands, plus educational programmes, licensing, buzz and promotional activity. Some of this is focused on recruiting new users, but more and more we are trying to reinforce the loyalty of our existing customers. We do this worldwide but largely on a local basis in order that we maintain the very human, intimate relationship which we have with our users.

We are also like any other media owner in that we have our direct customers (readers, viewers, listeners) who are our lifeblood but it is our advertisers and online retailers who provide our revenue. We are spending more and more time building relationships with these partners so they understand the dynamics of the Yahoo! brand and we understand their requirements from Yahoo!

Over the last few years, we have developed true partnerships that go beyond that of a traditional media owner relationship, providing real value to both companies. Examples include pairing up with Kmart to launch their Bluelight ISP and supporting education initiatives to the mass audience, and pairing up with Pepsi to launch an integrated on- and offline joint promotion driving young kids to purchase Pepsi and redeem loyalty points accrued on Pepsi merchandise hosted on Yahoo!

The future

Now we have established Yahoo! as a global brand, our key challenge is to maintain the momentum of growth. Here we are helped by technology as well as by our own ambitions. In many markets outside North America, Internet usage is still in its development stages and growing rapidly. In addition, the emergence of new platforms such as WAP mobile phone and Internet access via the TV will drive usage and penetration.

The WAP-enabled mobile phone will reach consumers in many markets that have limited PC access and poor wired telecommunications. This is particularly true in southern Europe, which is fast-tracking Internet access. We expect a similar outcome in Latin America and in much of Asia. Digital TV and its promise of true interactivity is another new platform set to drive Internet penetration. For example, both the leading UK digital TV players – On Digital and Open – are planning to open up their systems with Internet access by the end of 2000. Interactive television will provide a major new market for people without PCs who are currently unused to the Net.

A final factor in accelerating the uptake of the Internet outside North America is that, as expected, bigger companies have been embracing the Internet first – and there is much evidence to prove that big companies are driving a lot of new traffic onto the Internet. Smaller businesses (SMEs), however, have taken time to invest in and create the technological infrastructure to make workplace Internet – and intranet use – the norm. A key driver has been application service provision which is increasingly being made available to SMEs via the Net. Another driver has, of course, been e-mail. Away from the workplace, many of these smaller companies are exploring opportunities to communicate both with customers and suppliers using the Net. The effect of electronic transactions and e-communication on corporate culture is also having a knock-on effect on individual employees' desire and willingness to use the Internet in the office and at home. Yahoo! is well positioned to attract users in the SME sector, since their entrepreneurial spirit is at one with our own values.

So we expect these factors to drive the current trend towards a broadening of Internet use – both in terms of who is using the Net, and how. Tomorrow's generation of surfers will not just be using the Internet from the office using desktop PCs – the current norm. Increasingly, we will see much more Internet use from home – both using home computers and via interactive TV. And we will see Internet use on the move – thanks to evolving mobile phone technology, which will herald the birth of a whole new generation of mobile, personal communications devices. Yahoo! will be there to serve these new users, just as we were at the very start of the World Wide Web.

Commentary

Yahoo! is to some extent a brand that 'happened'. Certainly its founders did not intend to create a brand. On the other hand they were quick to realize that 'David and Jerry's Guide to the Web' was not exactly snappy or memorable. They were equally quick to recognize the need for professional marketing management once the brand began to take off.

Yahoo! is an excellent example of managing international expansion in a disciplined way, without creating a straitjacket which discourages local management. Here is a brand with some distinctive universal values which are easily understood yet with enough freedom to ensure they tap into local culture as they expand. They are, of course, helped in the youthful bias of Internet users. The newness of the Net itself means that there are some global values which individuals everywhere can embrace for these sort of products. This will be true for many technology driven brands in the future.

Yahoo! also demonstrates the speed with which a brand can be created in the modern world and how fundamental values like trust and honesty can be built into a brand very quickly.

Glossary

Brand architecture – the strategic relationship between the brands

Brand capital – the value of the business that exists beyond physical assets, technology and financial revenues

Brand communication equities – the 'ownable' brand communication assets that reflect the brand ideology and could be any number of the following: a logo, a strapline, a series of works, a visual language used in every context, a particular colour or colours, a sound, a packaging shape or material, the architecture of the retail outlets, the physical design of the product

Brand positioning – what does the brand stand for? And, in what way does it stand out?

Brand shifting^{TM} – the term created by Springpoint to describe the movement of the positioning and definition of the business you are in

CEqs^{TM} – Brand communication equities

NVD – New venture development

Soft values, the intangibles: – the values employees believe in which are brought to life through the brand and assimilated in the business plan

Index